Praise for *In the Trenches*

"Kelsey Gillespy's book is like a warm cup of cocoa for the weary mother's soul. Kelsey combines practical advice with the kind tone of a dear friend. I just wish I'd had this book when my own children were little!"

— Jen Fulwiler, standup comic and bestselling author

"With humor and grace, Kelsey Gillespy calls out the daily opportunities for holiness hidden in the trenches of early parenthood. Her reflections are an inspired invitation to a deeper relationship with God in what might seem an unlikely stage of life. Every new and expecting mother needs this book!"

— Lindsay Schlegel, author of *Don't Forget to Say Thank You: And Other Parenting Lessons That Brought Me Closer to God*

"As a Catholic mom of five young boys, I cannot recommend *In the Trenches* enough! Kelsey articulates the modern universal struggles of early motherhood in such a relatable way, leaving the reader with profound hope for the journey. I found myself laughing and crying through the chapters, wanting to highlight every word of her prayers! I would highly recommend this book to all moms wanting faithful encouragement in motherhood. Thank you, Kelsey, for putting so beautifully into words what our mama hearts need!"

— Alex DeRose, Instagrammer and blogger for
JoyMamaBlog.com

"*In the Trenches* provides a refreshing perspective on the vocation of motherhood. Gillespy offers solidarity through real-life events of the trenches experienced as mothers. This book is not just another attempt to discover the secret formula to parenting. It offers prayer, reflection, and acceptance of the beautiful season of motherhood the reader finds herself in."

— Steph Salinas, Director of Events and Spanish Ministry
for Blessed Is She

"Kelsey Gillespy draws upon her own motherhood to shine a light of hope into the desolation that can sometimes come during parenting. Her thoughtful reflections make for beautiful meditations upon God and his love."

— Gloria Purvis, speaker, author, and host and executive
producer of *The Gloria Purvis Podcast*

in the Trenches

Finding God Through Parenting Littles

By Kelsey Gillespy

Pauline
BOOKS & MEDIA
BOSTON

Library of Congress Cataloging-in-Publication Data Number: 2022943332.

CIP Data is available.

ISBN 0-8198-3752-0
ISBN 978-0-8198-3752-3

The Scripture quotations contained herein are from the *New Revised Standard Version Bible: Catholic Edition*, copyright © 1989, 1993, National Council of the Churches of Christ in the United States of America. Used by permission. All rights reserved worldwide.

Cover design by Tisa Muico

"P" and PAULINE are registered trademarks of the Daughters of St. Paul.

Published by Pauline Books & Media, 50 Saint Pauls Avenue, Boston, MA 02130–3491

Printed in the U.S.A.

www.pauline.org

Pauline Books & Media is the publishing house of the Daughters of St. Paul, an international congregation of women religious serving the Church with the communications media.

1 2 3 4 5 6 7 8 9   27 26 25 24 23

To every mother who has ever felt
exhausted, invisible, or alone,
especially my own mother,
who fought in the trenches
with unceasing love

Contents

PART II
WHO IS GOD?

PART IV

YOU CAN HAVE IT ALL WITHOUT WAITING
"UNTIL THEY'RE OLDER"

Introduction

Hi, Friend! How Old Are You?

My kids make friends everywhere they go. It could be at the playground or in dance class or in line at the grocery store. One time they even played with friends in a public restroom. Every encounter sounds something like this:

My kid: Hi, friend!

Other kid: Hi.

My kid: How old are you?

Other kid: (Says a number)

My kid: (Gasps audibly) I know somebody who's that old! Let's play!

Then they go running off together, beaming with joy. Sometimes they end up sitting on top of the monkey bars, chatting like little birds. Other times, they land in the sandbox. Still others, they chase each other around, shrieking and laughing all the while.

Later, my kids come running to me, red-faced and thirsty, dying to tell me everything they know about their new bestie. The in-depth reports usually include how old that friend was and *maybe* their birthday. If

1

I'm really lucky, I get a description of how tall they were, too.

"What was their name?" I ask every single time.

They shrug. "I don't know, but can we play with them again sometime?"

This tactic seems to work like a charm (my daughter even picked up a boy's mom's phone number this way so we could have a play date), but I'm not sure if it would fly in adult relationships. So, I won't ask how old you are or invite you into a filthy sandbox. But I would like to be friends.

So, let's see how this works . . .

Hi, friend! I'm Kelsey. I'm a mom by trade, professional toddler-wrangler and bottom-wiper by practice. There's nothing exceptional about me aside from the fact that I birthed five children in nine years and lived to tell about it. I don't have a PhD (though I *do* have a Master's Degree in Sport Psychology). I don't have celebrity status (though to my kids, that might be a different story). I don't have millions of dollars or a huge, cultlike following. The most valuable thing I have is my experience as a mother, which, as it turns out, is more valuable than I originally thought.

You see, I grew up in the Midwest in a stereotypical suburban family. The only thing we were lacking was a picket fence. My mom stayed at home with my brother and me and set the standard as an extremely engaged and invested mother who constantly put her family first. But one time, as we played a game I undoubtedly chose, she paused and looked down at me. Fatigue clouded her eyes. Her brow pinched in longing.

She sighed. "It's lonely being a mom."

At the time, I didn't know how to respond. How could she be lonely when I was always right there with her? I mean, really. I never left her side. What more could she want? To me, it seemed like being a mom was the best gig in the world. She got to play with me—the kid she surely adored more than anything else in life—every single day. No breaks, no exceptions. What could be better than that?

But still, her words stuck with me. Years passed. Then decades. Slowly, the Velcro that attached me to her wore down and I was able to pull free and finally give her some space. Not that she ever asked me to.

Soon afterward, I gave birth to my first baby and I didn't see another adult face aside from my husband's for months. From the depths of my subconscious, my mother's words floated to mind.

It's lonely being a mom.

Finally, her words made sense. For the first several months of my baby's life, my daughter and I didn't leave the house. Instead, we stayed in the living room with all the blinds closed so no one could catch a glimpse of me trying to figure out how to breastfeed. Like a psychopath, I sat on the couch, rocking back and forth, singing one song over and over because that was the only thing that calmed the baby, and it was also all my exhausted brain could muster.

But I wasn't the only one who suffered from the new-parent level of exhaustion. Once, my husband shook me awake in the middle of the night.

"Kelsey, you have to feed the baby."

I rubbed an eye and fought through the thick fog of sleep deprivation. Still, I couldn't understand what he was saying. "What?"

"You have to feed the baby!" he said again, this time more urgently.

I absorbed his panic, the hazy cloud in my head now completely gone as my heart raced in my chest. "Where is she?"

"I just gave her to you!"

"You *what*?" The panic kicked into full gear. I didn't remember getting the baby from him. All I knew was that I didn't have a baby in my hands. Or in my lap. DID I DROP HER? *Oh God, please tell me I didn't drop my baby!* I desperately searched all around—on the floor, under the blankets, everywhere. I smoothed my hand on top of the blankets, trying to feel for her in the dark. Instead, my fingers found something soft and glossy.

I picked it up and examined it closer in the moonlight. It was a pair of my husband's athletic shorts.

"How the heck did these get in here?" I said, holding them up so my husband could see.

Even in the darkness, I could see his face flush. Somehow, through sleep and dreams and fatigue, he had walked to his dresser, pulled out a pair of shorts thinking it was the baby, and wanted me to feed them.

Sure enough, when we looked, the baby was sound asleep in her crib beside our bed.

It was a crazy moment for sure, and I can promise it wasn't the last. But now, as we look back on those moments, we laugh. Now—years later—those moments are remembered with joy because we accompanied each other in the trenches of parenthood. And man, these trenches can be pretty deep and dark. I know because I've been there, surrounded by the shadows and loneliness. I've seen my own mother swallowed by their depth, and I've witnessed and walked with other moms who've said the same thing.

It's lonely being a mom.

So often we fight alone, keeping our heads down, grinding through these days just to get them over with. Past the temper tantrums and blowout diapers. Beyond the middle-of-the-night feedings and early-morning wake-up calls.

Slowly, surely, we climb to the top of the trench, throw one arm over the ledge, then the other, and pull ourselves out. But that takes years. Years of formative growth for our children, no doubt, but also years that can be formative growth for *us* if we allow them to be.

What if we could *enjoy* these trenches? What if we could work together, hand in hand? What if by talking to other moms (or reading this book), you discovered that these trenches can be surprisingly beautiful? And, most importantly, instead of making you lose your identity and grow stale in your relationship with God, what if these years could fill you up and make your faith grow?

Well, that's why I'm writing this book. For you. To show you that you're not alone, though you may feel like it sometimes. This book is my attempt to rise from the muck, to walk through these trenches and look in the eyes of all of you who are in here with me. This book is to let you know I *see* you. I see you sacrificing sleep to feed your baby or strip pee-soaked sheets from small beds. I see you changing diapers and wearing day-old spit up. I see you getting shouted at by an angry toddler and trying your hardest not to lose your mind. I see you giving even when you feel like you have nothing left to give. And yes, I can even see (and understand) the moments of saying and doing things you regret (girl, been there).

Parenthood forces us to set ourselves aside, that's true. It calls us to immense selflessness. But that doesn't mean you must disappear or be forgotten.

This book will tell you that you are valuable.

You're not alone.

You're just in the trenches.

And I'm right here with you.

By reading this book, you are choosing community. You are choosing solidarity. You are choosing to stop grinding this whole motherhood thing out on your own, and instead, you are bravely rising to your feet to walk beside all the others who are in these trenches with you. As you continue reading, I encourage you to take your time and prayerfully reflect on the following sections. Go so far as to write those reflections in a prayer journal. In fact, why don't you grab that right now? Get a pen or pencil while you're up, too. Seriously.

I'll wait.

Back already? Awesome.

As I was saying, this book is meant to be a tool for your own personal use. It's not a race. You don't have to sprint through. It's more of a walk. A journey, really. So take your time. Use the following sections and reflections however they may be most beneficial to you. You can go from the beginning to end, one chapter a day, to become a holier and more whole mother in a month. Or, if there's a section that speaks most to you, you can spend time really digging into it. However you decide to use it, this book is designed to help you claim your own identity, grow richer in your faith, and live your vocation as a mother to its fullest.

Together, we'll find the true purpose and meaning of parenthood, examine the characteristics of God, discover who *you* really are, and figure out how the heck you can have a rich faith and sense of identity *while* doing the mom thing. Whew. Sounds like a lot. But really, it's pretty simple. We'll walk through all of that together, one step at a time. Here's what you'll find in every chapter:

Scripture Verse: hear what God has to say about that chapter's reflection.

Real Life Stories: read stories from my own crazy life as a mother that have taught me more about God.

Snack Time!: nibble on a thought, suggestion, and/ or question that will nourish and sustain you throughout the day.

Prayer: bring it all back to God through prayer.

Further reflection and group discussion questions are located in the back of this book, in case some sort of miracle occurs and you find extra time to dive deeper on your own or meet with your group of gals on the weekend. (It probably wouldn't be this weekend, of course. No mom is free on that short of a notice. But maybe in, like, thirteen weekends when a few of you can find a spare hour.) Whatever happens, deeper reflection guides are there if you need them, and you can reference them whenever you feel inclined to do so.

I am so excited to walk with you, both in the pages of this book and in the trenches of this life. Maybe someday we'll meet in person and can share more of our stories, some with laughter, some with tears. All of them, no doubt, over a cup of something caffeinated. Whatever the case, I hope you know that you are surrounded by a community of women (including me!) who share similar hopes, dreams, and struggles. Now, as you continue to put one foot in front of the other, remember that you are covered in my prayers and the unblemished intercession of the saints, so that you may love your vocation and live it to its fullest.

PART I

What Is Parenthood?

1

"You're in the Trenches"

The Exhaustion and Loneliness of Motherhood

"Let us not grow weary in doing what is right, for we will reap at harvest time, if we do not give up" (Galatians 6:9).

"FOUR?" The woman's eyes nearly popped out of her head, which was quite an understandable response.

I hadn't showered in days, and I had barely slept during that time because that's what happens when you've just had your fourth baby in six years. So, I crouched there in the dance studio lobby looking half dead, shoving my daughter's feet into some too-small tap shoes. I only knew what day it was because that happened to be the day of the week when I took my daughters to dance class and tried to entertain all my littles.

In one small room.

For two hours.

With a huff, I rose to my feet and watched my daughter skip into the studio.

"Four," I echoed, and silently counted each one of my kids to make sure they were all there. It wasn't too hard. One was in class. The others were all hanging from my body.

My oldest cackled as she climbed my torso, my two-year-old clung shyly to my leg, and the newborn screamed from her car seat, which was dangling from the crook of my elbow.

We had only been there a little while and I was already on the verge of collapse.

Tightness squeezed my chest. Managing the chaos at home was hard enough. But having them all together in one crowded, public space? I took a deep breath and checked my watch. Thanks to being 10 minutes late, we only had 110 minutes to go.

The other mom finally blinked. "I bet you can't wait for school to start again."

"Actually," I said, shooing my oldest off my waist, "we homeschool."

Her jaw dropped. I didn't blame her for it. "You *homeschool*?"

"That's right." I set the baby down, shuffled to the nearest chair with my toddler still attached to my leg, and then started to fish through my bag for my nursing cover. Instead, I found some diapers and some wipes.

An extra pair of infant clothes. A grocery bag. Snacks. All the water cups for my big kids. Somehow even a squeaky toy was in there. My heart raced inside my chest as heat surged into my cheeks. *Please tell me I packed my nursing cover.* I stuck my head inside the bag and looked around, finally finding the floral cloth at the bottom of the bag. Flinging the loop around my head, I tucked the newborn beneath the cover and took a breath.

"You must never get a break," another woman piped up.

My head jerked in her direction. The constant noise and chaos of life had made coherent thoughts difficult over the past several years. But in that moment, when my scattered thoughts and bedraggled emotions were all jumbled up and put together, I realized that they echoed her words exactly.

I never got a break.

Not in the morning when I first opened my eyes. Not all day long. Not even in the middle of the night.

Never.

I glanced back at the woman as she chucked a Cheeto in her mouth and then handed one to her daughter. She didn't have to utter another syllable. She understood. I could see it in her tired smile, in the way her bag overflowed with prepacked snacks and pint-sized clothes, in the tiny wrinkles cupping her eyes and lips—marks left behind by laughter and fatigue and worry.

We were women who were constantly watched, but rarely *seen*. Constantly criticized, and yet always overlooked.

Moms.

We were moms.

Exhausted. Overwhelmed. Full of obligations and demands.

And we never got a break.

But what exactly was I wanting a break *from*? My children? Their personalities? Motherhood in general?

I wrestled with that question as I patted my baby's back.

Would a good mother want a break from her children? *Bounce, bounce.*

Is that what I really want? *Pat, pat.*

To be away from them? *Pat, pat.*

I love them, I really do. I'm just so exhausted that—*BURP!*

A bright white stripe of smelly, partially digested milk ran down the front of my shirt, splotching the chair beneath me and puddling on the floor. The baby screamed in my face as I whipped out the wipes and started scrubbing spit up off the dance studio's furniture, commanding my big kids to stay away from the mess.

This. This was what I needed a break from.

Not motherhood, but the feeling of being alone in its grind. From being all by myself in these trenches.

Invisible. Scrapping to survive. Caked in dirt and the smell of human waste. Buried in tears and bloodcurdling screams.

"My kids were spit-uppers, too," Cheeto Mom said. "They had to take medicine it got so bad."

Her words extinguished the flames in my cheeks. Suddenly, the mess wasn't an embarrassment. It was a bridge. A connection to someone else in the trench.

And *that* was what I needed. Ironically, my baby's vomit was the key to getting the break I craved.

I tucked the spit-up soaked wipe back in my diaper bag and struck up a conversation with Cheeto Mom. As we talked, our kids began playing together on the freshly cleaned floor, and the anxiety in my chest disappeared. We chatted about motherhood, temper tantrums, and sleep deprivation. We connected about our kids' education and activities. We talked about our husbands and jobs and how we would survive another day.

Before I knew it, dance class was over, and my daughter raced over to jump into my arms. I squeezed her tight before scooping up the baby, who was now snoozing in her car seat.

Silently, I counted my kids to make sure they were all there. It wasn't too hard. They were all, in some way, hanging from my body.

"Ready?" my daughter asked in her innocent, high-pitched voice.

I nodded.

Then, step by tiny toddler step, we slowly crossed the street.

But this time, as my children clung to me, the load felt like one I could carry.

SNACK TIME!

Making connections with other moms in the trenches is essential. How can you reach out to another mom today?

PRAYER

Jesus, these trenches of motherhood feel so lonely and exhausting. I can barely rise from the floor, let alone get up and walk through these dank tunnels. Yet over and over in Scripture, that's what you tell people to do. Rise and walk. It's a product of your divine healing. Lord, heal me of my spiritual and physical fatigue. Be the remedy for my loneliness. Then reach your all-powerful hand out to me and help me rise and walk through these trenches. Help me encounter other moms who are in here with me. We all need each other, Lord, and, more than anything, we all need you. Amen.

2

"Growing Like a Weed"

Nurturing Virtue and Uprooting Vice

"But as for what was sown on good soil, this is the one who hears the word and understands it, who indeed bears fruit and yields, in one case a hundredfold, in another sixty, and in another thirty" (Matthew 13:23).

My thumb has never been green.

Every plant I've cared for has quickly wilted, paled, and keeled over.

So it was a big surprise (to myself and my children) when I requested a plot in the community garden at our local library.

I didn't know the first thing about gardening. I didn't know about proper soil, sunlight, or water. I didn't know what kinds of tools to use. I didn't even know what to look for when (or if) seedlings began to sprout.

So, as I walked into the garden that was buzzing with bees and my children's abundant energy, I kicked myself. Why had I done this? I was clueless. But we were there. There was no going back now. So, with my God-given hardheadedness, I put my chin down and pressed forward, determined to learn.

Fortunately, when we passed the wooden gate around the perimeter, we saw the director of the garden bending over the compost pile. Through our communications, he already knew we were newbies who understood nothing about gardening.

"Don't worry," he said in a calm, understanding manner. "You're going to make lots of mistakes, and that's okay."

Somehow, being expected to mess up made me feel better. It took the pressure off a bit. I glanced at our lifeless plot—a rectangular blank slate filled with dirt and weeds—and had no idea where to begin.

The director told us to start by pulling up the old weeds and roots.

With adult-sized gloves flopping over their tiny fingers, my kids squealed with delight at the chance to play in dirt. Bucketful by bucketful, we emptied waste from our section of the garden and dumped it into the trash.

Before long, the dry, rocky dirt had transformed into dark, rich soil. I was shocked. Was this really the same plot of land?

The director came back over to inspect it. He grabbed a handful of dirt and sifted it through his fingers. "Wow," he said, his eyebrows arched in surprise. "You're definitely ready for sowing now."

He walked us through everything, step-by-step. He told us what kinds of plants flourished at that time of year. He showed us how to make neat rows with our fingers. He taught us how deep each seed must be planted for optimal growth.

He taught us everything. Without him, we'd be lost. There's no doubt about that.

Even now, I find myself looking for him when we go back to check on our plants. More often than not, his only advice is to water the soil, trim the weeds, and then wait and let the sun do its work.

Isn't that just like parenthood? Especially in the early years.

When my husband and I first found out we were pregnant, it was a big surprise to both of us.

I didn't know the first thing about parenting. I didn't know anything about breastfeeding or formula. I didn't know how to change a diaper. I didn't know what to do when babies got sick. Not to mention, I had no idea what to do when my babies would begin to grow and all the questions would evolve into bigger, harder questions.

So, as my husband and I crept ever closer to delivery, buzzing with nerves, I beat myself up a bit. Would a baby even survive under my care? I was clueless. But, with my God-given hardheadedness, I put my chin down and pressed forward, determined to learn.

Fortunately, I discovered, we have a God we can go to for guidance and help.

"Don't worry," he said in a calm, understanding manner. "You're going to make lots of mistakes, and that's okay."

Somehow, being expected to mess up made me feel better.

Still, I took a hard look at my life—this small space of the world where a new person would root and grow—and found it to be full of weeds. How would I make it suitable for someone else to flourish? I didn't even know where to begin.

First, God said, I had to pull up the old weeds and roots.

He took me through everything, step-by-step. He showed me how to die to myself to serve others. He taught me about humility, patience, and charity. He even went so far as to be present in his Church so I could be nourished by him in the Eucharist.

He's taught me everything I know. Without him, I'd be lost. There's no doubt about that.

I've spent years wrist-deep in dirt, sorting the good from the bad, pulling rocks and weeds out by the handful, searching for roots that could be harmful. Roots like the desire to think only of myself. The desire to get everything I want. The desire to go untouched for a moment. And, as my babies have grown into toddlers and young children, I find new weeds to yank on. Impatience. Quickness to anger. A flaring temper that, before kids, I didn't even know I had. Pull, pull, pull.

Bucketful by bucketful, I've emptied waste from my life and dumped it out.

And it's hard.

Even now, as I check on my children, I find myself looking for God, seeking advice. Sure enough, he's always there to give encouragement and instruction.

More often than not, his only advice is to water the soil, remove any weeds, and then let the Son do his work.

SNACK TIME!

Pluck a vice, plant a virtue.

PRAYER

Lord, you are the Master Gardener. Help me work together with you to clean up my heart and make it a pleasant home for you and those around me. Amen.

3

"Do As I Say, Not As I Do"

Accepting What God Has Given You

"For I, the Lord your God,
 hold your right hand;
it is I who say to you, 'Do not fear,
 I will help you'" (Isaiah 41:13).

Thursday means one thing at our house.

Pizza.

I won't say how long we've held the tradition of grabbing a greasy pizza once a week, but I will say it has been such a beloved, time-tested tradition in our family that one of my son's first words was "pizza."

Back then, he hung from the crook of my elbow in his car seat as I paid for our pre-ordered meal.

"EEEEEEETTTZZZAAAAAAAA!!!!" he'd shout, his high-pitched voice rising above the ringing phones, the bantering employees, the roar of the oven. "EEETZA! EEETZA! EEETZAAAAAA!!!!"

Once, an employee stopped everything he was doing to cock a brow at the little baby. Then he turned his confused look to me. "Is that baby yelling, 'pizza'?"

Flushing, I casually flicked my wrist, as though it were totally normal for babies to have an addiction to greasy food. "He really likes pizza."

And it continued that way for a long time. The boy ate so much pizza in one sitting, his cheeks were stained red from tomato sauce.

Now, at three years old, my son still loves pizza.

So it isn't any wonder that, not too many Thursdays ago, he came to the pizza parlor with me and his baby sister to pick up a big ol' pie.

"All right, bud, I'm going to need your help," I said as I gathered all our things together.

Eagerly, he leapt to my side, ready for action. "What can I do to help?"

I plopped three containers of extra sauces into his hands. "I need you to carry these."

Three sauces. Two small hands.

His jaw dropped in disbelief. "You mean I have to carry ALL the sauces?"

"Yes, that would be very helpful," I replied as I slung the diaper bag over one shoulder and picked up the baby in her car seat. And also got the pizza. And the breadsticks. *And* opened the door so my son could walk through. And. And. And.

My son followed, grimacing in intense concentration as he stared down the full load in his hands. Gingerly, he walked to the van, taking one slow step. Then another. Aaaaaand another. Careful not to drop what he'd been given. Finally—thank heavens—we were at the car door.

Is that what I look like when God asks me to do something? I wondered, a smile half-cocked on my face as my son dumped all the sauces in the passenger seat and then grumbled about how much he had to do.

The answer was yes. That's exactly what I look like.

Every day, God plops some extremely minuscule portion of his will into my hands.

I feel its weight in my clumsy fingers, and almost instantly, my jaw drops in disbelief.

You mean I have to take care of ALL these kids?

You mean I have to do ALL this laundry?

You mean I have to wash ALL these dishes?

You mean I have to write ALL these chapters?

"Yes, that would be very helpful," God replies, humbly leaving out the fact that he was the One who created the kids. And gave me an amazing, supportive husband. And provided our clothes, our home, our washing machine, our dishwasher, our dishes, our *everything*. And gave me the ideas and inspiration for my writing. And opened the doors for me to pursue writing. And. And. And.

I follow him as best I can, grimacing in intense concentration as I stare down the full load in my hands. Gingerly, I walk beside him, taking one slow step. Then another. And another. Careful not to drop what little I've been given.

Finally, thank heavens, I reach the end of the day and let everything drop, astounded by how much I got accomplished.

Yet, in reality, I hold the smallest fraction of the big picture. God knows I can't hold the big stuff. It would flatten me outright. So he does the heavy lifting, walking beside me, matching my extremely slow stride as I fumble the tiny bit in my hands. Struggling to take each. Slow. Step.

The truth is, it would probably be easier for God if he just did everything and we got out of his way.

But, for whatever reason, he made us to be helpers. Co-redeemers.

All we have to do is hold the sauce and walk with him.

SNACK TIME!

Take your eyes off your sauce for a second and look for the things God is taking care of for you.

PRAYER

You, Lord, are almighty, omnipotent, and omnipresent. I am none of those things. Though I try to do it all, I get weary. Though I want to do my best, I often feel incompetent. Though I'm often stretched in several directions, I quickly learn I cannot be in more than one place at one time. God, when I feel overwhelmed with the portion you've given me, take my hand in yours and help me. Let me never forget that you walk with me and take care of more than I could ever possibly imagine. Give me a heart that seeks you always and praises you for the mighty works you are constantly doing in my life. Amen.

4

"There's a Method to My Madness"

When God's Will Isn't Glamorous

"Live for the rest of your earthly life no longer by human desires but by the will of God" (1 Peter 4:2).

My two-year-old has a strange infatuation with the dishwasher. She loves soap pods, sharp utensils, and delicate glassware.

"Mommy help," she calls it. (Which is not to be confused with her *asking* for help, which sounds more like, "Mommy, help.")

Usually, I try to race through finishing the dishes before she realizes what I'm doing, but the *clank clank* of ceramic plates is a siren song to her ears. She can't help but be lured into the kitchen.

So, as I collected the plates out of the dishwasher the other day, I wasn't surprised to hear the pitter-patter of two tiny feet sprinting across the tile toward the kitchen.

Welp, I shrugged to myself, *looks like she gets to help today.*

She rounded the kitchen corner and raced toward the dishwasher, a smile exploding across her sweet face, her hands poised to grab something breakable. "Mommy help!" she exclaimed.

I chuckled at her eagerness. "Of course you can help."

The little girl squealed with delight.

At that moment, I noticed a couple crumpled paper towels lying on the counter. "You know what would be really helpful?" I said sincerely, picking up the white rectangles, scrunching them smaller, then holding them out to her. "It would be really helpful if you put these paper towels in the trash can for me."

My daughter's jaw dropped. "No!" she shouted, her eyes bulging with shocked hurt. "Mommy help!"

"I love that you want to help me, but the most helpful thing you can do now is put these paper towels in the trash can."

At first, she resisted, thinking the only way to help me was to do things her own way. Eventually, though, she took the soiled towels and tossed them in the garbage.

"Yay!" I cheered, genuinely grateful that the towels were off the counter and where they belonged. My daughter clapped her pudgy palms together to cheer for herself, too.

She gets it from me, that thing about helping in the way *she* wants to help.

You see, I have this strange infatuation with writing. I love slipping away to cafes, the smell of roasted coffee beans swirling with my thoughts as I drink something hot from a thick mug.

I find myself sprinting to my laptop, a smile exploding across my face, my hands poised on the keys, ready to start tap-tap-tapping away. Before I begin, I ask God how I can help him, pleading to be used in a meaningful way.

He must chuckle at my eagerness. "Of course you can help."

I squeal with delight because, in my mind, helping God looks like writing while sipping something caffeinated. Untouched. Alone with my thoughts. For hours. The hiss of steaming milk is like a siren song to my ears, and I can't help but feel lured through the front door of the local coffee shop.

But that's not always how God asks me to help.

Sometimes God's will isn't glamorous. It's not what I thought it'd be.

Sometimes, instead of getting up early to write, I find that God has asked me to stay awake all night, washing vomit off a kid and all the bed sheets.

Sometimes, as my fingers are itching to get to the keyboard, God wants me to listen to a kid's completely made-up dream for eight minutes straight.

Sometimes I get up early to write, but all the kids wake up, too, so God asks me to make breakfast instead.

The first time he asked me to do those things, my jaw dropped. "No!" I shouted, my eyes bulging with shocked hurt. "I want to help you!"

"I love that you want to help me, but those are the most helpful things you can do right now."

At first, I resisted, thinking the only way to help God was to do things my own way. I even *resented* those menial, detestable tasks God was asking me to do. After all, they were keeping me from the amazing works I could do for God—all the amazing things I could *be*—if only I had the chance to go *do* them.

But, eventually, I took his direction and did the things he was asking of me.

Beside me, he cheered, genuinely grateful that I was willing to do what needed to be done to make his kingdom come. To show his love and put it into action. To be visible, tangible proof that he really exists.

You see, God's will is not always pretty, but it is still God's will. It's still what he's asking us to do. It's truly the most helpful thing we could do for him.

And that makes it more beautiful than anything else we could dream of on our own.

SNACK TIME!

God's will for your life includes what's happening today. Easy or difficult. Glamorous or not. How is he asking you to help him right now?

PRAYER

God, place in my heart a genuine desire to serve you, to please you, and to have a part in making your kingdom come, however that may look. Cast out my preconceptions of what it looks like to help you and inspire me to be firmly resolved to do whatever you ask of me. Even if it's not my favorite thing. Even if it's dirty and tiring. Even if it seems menial and mind-numbing. Let me not resist, but rather rejoice in the tasks you give me—because I'm doing them for you. Amen.

5

"When You're a Parent, You'll Understand"

The Corporal Works of Mercy

"And the king will answer them, 'Truly I tell you, just as you did it to one of the least of these who are members of my family, you did it to me'" (Matthew 25:40).

My son's cry rattles me from sleep. I rub one eye and take a dreaded peek at the clock.

4:43.

Sigh.

Who needs alarms when they've got kids?

Tossing back the covers, I shiver in the chilly, predawn air. But this is it. No more covers. No more sleep. The baby's awake, the day's begun.

I slip into his room silently, though it's not like it matters. His wails have grown stronger and more desperate. Behind the bars, tears stain his sheets and crib mattress. I lift him over the railing and cradle him, absorbing the warmth of his small body. He nuzzles into me, rubbing his face against my pajama shirt. When he pulls back, a trail of mucus shines from my shoulder.

I grimace. "Did you just wipe your nose on me?"

He coughs uncontrollably in my face and I have my answer.

After wiping the germy spit from my cheeks, I collapse onto the recliner tucked in the corner of the nursery.

Maybe I can snag a few more minutes of sleep while he eats.

But before I can finish that thought, the door to my daughters' bedroom creaks open, followed by the sound of uncertain, shuffling feet and the unmistakable swish-swish of Pull-Ups on the prowl.

My two-year-old peeks her head into the nursery, allured by the soft blue light of the glowing lamp. The *only* light at this time of day.

"Mom?" She rubs a tired eye. "I'm hungry."

I let go of any hope of closing my eyes. "Okay, let me finish feeding your brother, and then—"

"And I'm wet."

With the baby still attached and slurping, I crouch beside my toddler and strip pee-soaked clothes from her body. She wraps her arms around herself and shivers.

"Now I'm cold, Mom!"

"I know." I suppress the frustrated huff rising into my throat. "Let's go get you some clothes."

"But I'm COLD!"

My heart pounds against my temples.

I glance at my daughter, the tiny girl with gigantic emotions. If she goes to get her own clothes, her flaring temper will surely wake her older sister, who shares the same bedroom.

I sigh. "Stay here. I'll get your clothes."

Fumbling through the dark, I make my way to the girls' room and open the dresser drawer. Slowly. Quietly. I reach inside, grabbing blindly, then go back to the nursery and slip the dry clothes onto my quivering daughter.

"Will you make some breakfast now, please?" she asks.

"Sure." I prop the baby onto my shoulder and pat his back as we walk downstairs. In response, he coughs in my face again.

As I fill bowls with cereal, my oldest comes out of her room, her hair a tangled mess, a shy grin glowing on her face. She scurries to me and presses her face into my abdomen.

"Good morning," she says, her soft words muffled by my shirt. "Can I have some milk in a cup, too, please?"

It's barely six o'clock and I already feel like a ragged, worked-to-death servant.

The word leaves a bitter taste in my mouth. *Servant.* Blech.

I could do so much more. *Be* so much more. If only I didn't have to wait kitchen tables and the small children crammed in the chairs.

But Jesus didn't call us to be comfortable. He never offered an easy, convenient life. And he definitely never promised prosperity in five fun DIY steps.

In fact, he did the opposite. He challenged us to do something way more difficult and counterintuitive. Something that's much harder to hear about and cheer for. He commanded us to die to ourselves. To be servants.

He told us to serve those who are without food and drink. To shelter people with nowhere to call home. To nurture, comfort, and heal the sick. To give company and mercy to those in prison. And even to give of our excess to those who need it more.

He calls us to live the Corporal Works of Mercy.

And parenthood—especially in the early years—is the embodiment of those works. Day after day after grueling, grinding day. We're constantly feeding the hungry and giving drink to the thirsty. Constantly clothing the naked and sheltering kids who otherwise would have nowhere to live. We tend our children when they're sick and help our babies who are imprisoned by both their cribs and their tiny bodies. And, at times, when God calls one of our babies Home, we mercifully bury the dead.

So, mommas, if you've been thinking that parenthood is tough, you're in good company. We are constantly dying to ourselves. Constantly meeting the needs of others while our own desires go unmet.

We are doing the greatest work on earth.

We are living as Jesus called us to live.

SNACK TIME!

How many of the Corporal Works of Mercy can you accomplish through your vocation as a mother today?

PRAYER

One day, I'll stand before you, Lord, wondering how I could possibly present myself—and all that I've done—to you.

You'll call my name, and I'll shrink at the sound, awaiting my judgement. You'll look at me, your eyes filled with Divine Mercy. "I was hungry and you fed me, thirsty and you gave me drink, naked and you clothed me, homeless and you sheltered me, imprisoned and you visited me."

"I did?" Confused, I'll raise my gaze from the ground, daring to look you in the face. "When?"

You'll flash your dazzling smile. "Don't you remember all the spilled bowls of cereal? The steam hissing over the stove as you cooked dinner? The whole first year of my life when you gave me milk? When I was born, I had no clothes. No place to lay my head. You gave me both. When I was in my crib, I cried out for you, and you came. Even when you were tired. Even when you had nothing else to give."

You'll pull me into a warm embrace, your life-giving breath in my hair, your voice no louder than a whisper. "Well done, good and faithful servant. Welcome Home."

6

"Use It or Lose It"

Showing Off Your Gifts to God

"Whatever your task, put yourselves into it, as done for the Lord and not for your masters" (Colossians 3:23).

"Mom, watch my new trick!" my three-year-old shouts. She's about to do something amazing. Or so she says.

I turn my focus toward her, and the small girl absorbs every ounce of my attention—a gift I hadn't realized was so precious—before she does it. Her trick. She has lots of them now. Spinning on one leg. Cartwheels. Falling face-first onto her mattress. Tumbling fearlessly off the couch into a tuck, roll, and finish.

I must admit, some of her "tricks" give my heart a slight hiccup. Still, I can't help but watch. I can't help but celebrate each new feat. These awkward gestures she is learning in her small body. This adult-sized ambition packed tightly into her toddler coordination and execution.

As her mother, I get to be there to cheer her on. To support her and encourage her to be bold. To try new things.

I'm grateful that it's *me* she wants as a witness.

And I truly delight in these new accomplishments. Even the simplest ones.

My youngest has caught on to this attention-grabbing technique.

"Look, Daddy!" she shouts, then twirls herself dizzy. Or runs as fast as she can on two stubby legs. Or celebrates that she put her fork on her plate when she wasn't using it.

She sticks out her tummy in triumph. Ta-da.

Look, Daddy.

My husband smiles and cheers, adoring his daughter's every move.

As he whoops and hollers, it occurs to me that I've never said those words to my own Father before.

Instead, I grind things out on my own, trying to please myself and those around me. By doing so, I stray from intentionally using my God-given abilities to actually please God.

I don't think much about showing him any new tricks. Heck, I don't think I have any. But even the smallest thing, if done for him, makes him rejoice.

So I turn my focus toward him now, absorbing every ounce of his attention—a gift I know to be infinitely precious—before I do it. My trick.

When I feel like I'm about to lose my temper with my kids, I will ask God for the grace of humility and slowness to anger.

Look, Daddy.

When I'm tired, I will still serve the family, however that needs to be done.

Look, Daddy.

When I am overwhelmed by the demands of work and motherhood, I will be present in the moment and show love before stress.

Look, Daddy.

When my kids soak their sheets or get scared in the middle of the night, I will put their need for love above my own need for sleep.

Look, Daddy.

When my family wants one thing, but I want another, I can yield to their request.

Look, Daddy.

When I'm tempted to bulldoze through life on my own strength, I will acknowledge the gifts and skills God has given me and use them for his glory.

Look, Daddy.

When I fail miserably at any or all of these things, I will depend on the graces of God to sustain me.

Look, Daddy.

And, as the loving Father that he is, he will celebrate these feats. These awkward gestures I am learning in my small body. This godly ambition packed tightly inside human execution.

He'll smile and cheer, adoring his daughter's every move.

He'll be grateful that it's *him* I want as a witness.

And, I hope to God, he'll truly delight in these actions. Even the simplest ones.

SNACK TIME!

What God-given gift can you show off to him today?

PRAYER

Lord God, you made me exactly as I am. Help me to rejoice in your creation and use your gifts for your glory. Let me never tire of trying to please you. Keep my eyes and heart fixed on you, Father. Remind me that my abilities are gifts from you and that to you they should return. Lord, as I pursue the path you've put before me, help me to remember that you're walking beside me every step of the way. May I never get so blinded by daily demands that I forget you're doing them with me. Amen.

7

"I've Got Eyes in the Back of My Head"

What to Do When You Feel Invisible

"Nathanael asked him, 'Where did you get to know me?' Jesus answered, 'I saw you under the fig tree before Philip called you'" (John 1:48).

One of my greatest joys is cheering for my kids when they do something amazing.

Amazing being a relative word, of course.

It could be writing a lowercase 'g' in the lines properly. Or swinging from the monkey bars. Or hopping around the room on one leg.

Amazing can quite literally mean anything.

Just last week, my almost-five-year-old daughter was in gymnastics class, and for some reason, they started juggling scarves. After a series of tricks, the coach asked them to toss a scarf into the air and try to catch it with their foot.

Well, let me tell you, my daughter is determined to a fault, even with something as trivial as catching scarves on her feet. (She gets it from her momma.)

So for a moment, she stood there, her brow furrowed in complete concentration as brightly colored patches of fabric floated around her through the air.

Finally, she tossed hers up and stuck out her foot. The scarf floated lazily back down.

Miss.

She tossed it again. Another miss.

Toss, toss. Miss. Miss.

Until, finally, the sheer square landed directly on the bridge of her tiny foot.

The smile that exploded across her face could have lit the entire gym. With twinkling blue eyes alive with accomplishment, she turned toward the coach.

But the coach wasn't looking.

And all her gymnast buddies were too focused to notice anything other than their own scarves.

I see you, sweet girl.

I raised my hands above my head victoriously in the viewing area, and my lips stretched into a wide smile as I tried to will her eyes to meet mine.

I see you.

But she never looked my way.

And a little kid can only balance on one leg for so long. Soon, she tipped over and the scarf sailed to the floor as though the trick never happened.

Everything about her—who she is, what she did—went seemingly unnoticed. Unappreciated.

Invisible.

Mommas, I don't know about you, but I feel like that all too often.

There are days—heck, even weeks and months—when it feels like I'm sprinting to take care of the physical, emotional, and spiritual needs of my family. Trying to clean the house, fold the laundry, do the dishes. Trying to write this book. Trying to get my post-baby body ready for physical exercise. Trying to stay close to Jesus amid the chaos.

Trying. Trying. Trying.

I'm constantly tossing scarves into the air and stretching in every direction to catch them on my foot.

And lots of times I miss.

But sometimes—just *sometimes*—I do something amazing.

Amazing being a relative word, of course.

It could be folding the laundry and miraculously getting all the clothes in the appropriate drawers. Or cooking three meals a day that everyone in my family actually eats. Or writing a chapter—or simply one sentence—that I'm proud of. Or, most amazing of all, playing with my kids without worrying about what task I need to take care of next.

With twinkling brown eyes alive with accomplishment, I turn toward my husband, my kids, my friends.

But sometimes they're not looking. Sometimes they're too focused on their own scarves to notice the one dangling from my foot.

And that's okay. It's not their job to keep their eyes on me.

But I can only balance my life for so long. Soon, I tip over and my scarf sails to the floor as though the amazing thing I did never happened.

Everything about me—who I am, what I did—feels unnoticed. Unappreciated.

Invisible.

Until I remember the viewing area. The one far outside my periphery.

Finally, I turn my attention in that direction. There my Father stands, his hands raised above his head victoriously. Turns out he's been there the whole time, watching, trying to will my eyes to meet his. His lips stretch into a wide smile as he says the words I've so longed to hear.

I see you, sweet girl. I see you.

SNACK TIME!

Look for the One who never takes his eyes off you.

PRAYER

Like Nathanael beneath the fig tree, I cry out to you, Lord. It seems as though every day is my fig tree. There are so many times I feel utterly alone and invisible. I try so hard and yet it all feels unnoticed or inadequate. I turn to you now, trusting in your word, believing when you tell me that you see me. Remind me that, as a Christian, it's not my job to be loved, but to be love. Then, with the help of the Holy Spirit, send me back into the world to love and serve my family, completely renewed and strengthened, knowing that you see me and rejoice. Amen.

8

"Were You Raised in a Barn? You're Filthy!"

The Purgatory of Parenthood

"He will sit as a refiner and purifier of silver, and he will purify . . . and refine them like gold and silver, until they present offerings to the LORD in righteousness" (Malachi 3:3).

My newborn hates diaper changes.

Especially when she's hungry.

If it were up to her, she'd happily sit in her mess, suckling milk until the waste burned holes on her bottom.

Even then—blistered and bleeding—she'd be contentedly milk-drunk, filled up with the one thing she'd wanted in this world.

But that wouldn't be good for her. So I have a different plan. A plan that involves changing her diaper before giving her any of her beloved milk.

And for the umpteenth time today, her diaper is full. (How on earth she manages to dirty herself this much, I don't know.) The familiar sogginess hangs from her bottom, its stench reaching my nose as I cradle her in my arms.

Because I love her, I pull her from the warm, comfy spot against my chest.

"You might get mad at me for this," I say as I lay her down.

Sure enough, her face flushes crimson as she struggles to breathe, choked by the intense despair of not getting what she wants. Tears gather at the corners of her eyes. Her bottom lip quivers. Those strong legs kick furiously.

The cold, hard table. The seemingly too-distant separation from Mom. The whole NO MILK thing.

It's all too much for her to bear.

I lift her up, wiping away the filth that would otherwise hurt her. They're a purgatory of sorts, these diaper changes. A preparatory and necessary cleansing. And to her, this doesn't always feel good.

"Just wait," I coo as she wails. "When you're all clean, you can actually enjoy what I have for you next."

The moment the words leave my lips, I hear God promise me the very same thing.

You see, this time with littles has been constant. Constant stretching in different directions. Constant sleeplessness. Constant harsh words and regret. Constant selfishness, flaring tempers, and impatience—all fractures in my soul I hadn't even known were there until I had little kids.

This season, I realized, is nothing more than a continual diaper change.

And, boy, do I hate diaper changes.

If it were up to me, I'd happily sit in my own mess, thinking only of myself until ignorant sin burned holes in my soul.

Even then—blistered and bleeding—I'd be contentedly oblivious, filled up with snacks and On Demand episodes of my favorite TV shows.

But that wouldn't purify or develop me in any way. In fact, sitting in front of a screen stuffing my mouth with sugar all the time wouldn't be good for me at all. So God's got a different plan.

A plan that involves cleaning me up before giving me the desires of my heart. A plan to sanctify me through mothering littles before giving me the next step on my journey. Teenagers? Then adults? Perhaps grandchildren one day? Heaven?

Whatever the next steps on my journey, my heart definitely needs to get cleaned up if I hope to walk them righteously.

So instead of blissfully sitting on my couch doing nothing to grow my spirit, I sit uncomfortably in the stink of my own anger and impatience for the umpteenth time today. (How on earth I manage to dirty myself this much, I don't know.) The familiar heaviness of my sin weighs on my heart, and I cringe at my own behavior—and boy, can *that* work wonders for the soul.

They are a purgatory of sorts, these trenches. A preparatory and necessary cleansing. And that doesn't always feel good.

Yet, over and over, God gently wipes away the filth that would otherwise hurt me.

When I must sacrifice my wants to tend to the needs of my kids, God wipes away my selfishness and allows humility to break through.

When I get my hands dirty in the mess of these trenches, God wipes away my aversions and gives me a glimpse of true charity.

When we need to leave the house, but my kids can't find their shoes for TEN FULL MINUTES, God wipes away my obsession with schedules and helps me grow in patience.

And when I kick and scream, refusing to let him perform these works in me, he *still* wipes me clean with the healing grace of the Eucharist and the sacrament of Confession.

"Just wait," he says while I wail. "When you're all clean, you can actually enjoy what I have for you next."

SNACK TIME!

How is God sanctifying you through motherhood?

PRAYER

O God, wipe away everything in me that is not of you. Clean me. Prepare my soul so that I may be more spiritually ready to embrace the vocation you have given me. At times, motherhood can seem so difficult. The physical demands wear me out and leave me spiritually dry. Help me to see this stage of life as a purgatory here on earth—a necessary cleansing of my selfishness, pride, and desire for comfort. It hurts to have those things scrubbed off. It's exhausting. At times, I want to cling desperately to them. Yet, remind me that if I let them go, my hands and heart will be open for you. Help me love these trenches for their constant purification of my soul. Put my heart in order, so I will want to be cleansed by you and rely more and more on your grace. Amen.

PART II

Who Is God?

9

"The Pot Calling the Kettle Black"

What God's Name Means

"'Look, the virgin shall conceive and bear a son,
    and they shall name him Emmanuel,'
which means, 'God is with us'" (Matthew 1:23).

I do not exist. At least, that's how I feel most days.

My older kids have entered this fun new stage where their ears have become deaf to the sound of my voice. It's as though my words are nothing but the wind. I could scream that the house was on fire and they'd still sit there, unflinching at the kitchen table, trying to decide if they should use "hot magenta" or "primrose" for the queen bunny's scepter in their coloring book.

It's only when they disagree, their frustration coming to punches and tears, that they come running to me, fingers pointing at each other in accusation, expecting me to condemn and punish the one who's in the wrong.

In the course of a single day, it's not uncommon for someone to run away from me and someone else to angrily chase me down. I've been both shouted at and given the silent treatment. I've been hugged and then slapped.

Because to my children, I'm merely whatever they want me to be. A judge. An executioner. A security blanket. A punching bag. A genie who will make whatever they want materialize in front of them.

But rarely, if ever, am I treated like the full person I am. A person with wishes and a heart for them. A person who wants the best for them. A person who dreams the lofty dream for her children to become saints.

And so they lose sight of the biggest part of my identity. They lose *me*.

"You know why you treat me like this?" I asked them on a particularly tough day. "Because I'm ALWAYS HERE!"

It was an inappropriate release of anger, really. An expression of my feeling trapped, caught in the chaos even when all I want to do is run away or sit alone crying in the closet.

But it's true.

I'm always here.

To me, those words can be suffocating. A lifelong prison sentence. An unbearable, impossible task. The part of my job description that's so all-consuming, it might as well be part of my name.

But in the same moment that I shouted those words at my children, God whispered them to me. You see, I've been in this stage lately where I haven't heard from my Father very much. It's not for his lack of trying, I'm sure. My ears have simply been deaf to his voice, as though his words were nothing but the wind. He could scream that my life was inflamed with sin, and I'd sit there, unflinching on my living room couch, trying to decide which movie to watch when the kids are in bed.

It's only when I'm angry or hurt, my frustration usually ending in tears, that I come sprinting to him.

In the course of a single day, it's not uncommon for me to run away from him and also to angrily chase him down. He's been both shouted at and given the silent treatment. Because to me, he becomes whatever I want him to be. A merciless judge. An executioner. A security blanket. A punching bag. A genie who can make whatever I want materialize in front of me.

But rarely do I treat the Father like the full Person that he is. A Person with wishes and a heart for me. A Person who wants the best for me. A Person who dreams the lofty dream for his child to become a saint.

And so I lose sight of the biggest part of his identity. I lose *him*.

"You know why you treat me like this?" he asks me. "Because I'm always here."

And it's true.

He's always here.

But to him, those words are a promise—a promise that takes on flesh in his Son. An eternal covenant. A profession of real, unconditional, unbreakable love. A description that is so dear to God, it is literally his Son's name.

Emmanuel.

God with us.

SNACK TIME!

Decide how you're going to treat the One who is always there for you.

PRAYER

How is it possible that you—the Almighty, the God who can literally do anything—willingly choose to use that power to be present in my life? God, please never let me take that for granted. Never let me overlook you. When you speak, give me ears to hear you. When you work in my life, give me eyes to see you and lips to praise you. Help me to receive the gift of your presence and show my gratitude by loving you to the best of my ability. Amen.

10

"Like Two Peas in a Pod"

Why God Chooses to Be with Us All the Time

"And remember, I am with you always, to the end of the age" (Matthew 28:20).

I stared in the mirror at the frothy white foam clinging to my lips.

What's so special about this? I wondered, spitting out the minty toothpaste and washing it down the sink. I peered around me. On this very rare occasion, I was alone. Standing in the quiet. Brushing my teeth. *There's nothing exciting about this, and yet God has promised he's here with me. At every moment. Always. But why on earth would he want to be here with me right now?*

I shook my head, answerless, wiped my face, flipped the lights off as I left the room, and then collapsed into bed beside my husband.

The following day, I took my son to gymnastics. Just me and him. A Mommy-Son date, as he likes to call it.

With the confidence of a young man but the strength of a little boy, he tugged and yanked and pulled the door open with all his might, and then ushered me through.

"Here you go," he said, nearly out of breath.

"How very helpful! Thank you, sir." I sailed through, smiling at him as he held the door with the entirety of his body weight.

He followed me inside, slipping his tiny hand into mine. "I like being with you, Mommy."

I playfully squeezed his hand in return. "I like being with you, too, sweet boy."

As usual, we were a few minutes late, so he quickly slipped off his wintery layers, socks, and shoes, stuffed everything into a cubby, and bolted into the gym. And, as usual, I stayed behind in the viewing area, watching as he bounded with glee toward his classmates.

During the hour my son is in gymnastics, I always stand by myself in the viewing area. There's no one calling for my attention. No hungry mouths begging for snacks. No diapers to change. There's just me. Waiting in the viewing area. I could do anything I want. I could sit on the bleachers and read a book or scroll mindlessly through my phone. I could catch up on emails or call a friend. Heck, I could leave altogether and go do something productive like grocery shop without tons of little kids running in tons of different directions.

But I don't.

I stand and I watch.

I watch as my son bounces straight up and down on the trampoline 427,402 times in a row. I watch when he climbs the matted steps to the parallel bars, which I know to be his favorite part of gymnastics. (The steps, that is. Not the bars.) I even keep my eyes fixed on him as he patiently sits in one spot waiting for his turn.

What's so special about this? The question echoed in my mind from the night before. *There's nothing exciting about watching little kids jump one inch off the floor over and over. So why on earth do I* want *to be here right now? Why do I feel like I can't take my eyes off him?*

And then, he did it.

He looked over at me and smiled.

In that moment—the half-second that it took for our eyes to lock—all my questions were answered.

I stay, my eyes fixed on my son, because on the off chance that he glances my way (which he does less and less as he gets comfortable in class), I want to be sure he finds me. I want him to know he's in my spotlight. I want him to know he's the most important thing in the world to me.

The same is true with God.

He stays, his eyes fixed on us, because on the off chance that we glance his way (which we do less and less as we get comfortable in the world), he wants to be sure we find him. He wants us to know we're in his spotlight. He wants us to know we're the most important thing in the world to him.

So often we slip our hand from his and bolt into our daily lives, attacking our schedules and the all-too-menial tasks that are set before us.

The breakfast routine. The getting kids to school or perhaps even teaching them ourselves.

The emails. The phone calls. The meetings.

The dishes. The laundry. The lunches, snacks, and dinners.

Heck, even the brushing of our teeth at the end of the night.

God is right there. Every moment. Always. Even when we don't notice him.

All because there's an off chance we might glance his way—a chance he might get to lock eyes with us—and *that* is the most exhilarating thing in the world.

SNACK TIME!

God is with you always, eagerly waiting for the chance to lock eyes with you. Can you find times during your day to turn your heart toward him?

PRAYER

God, you are so good. So faithful. How is it that you are mindful of me? That you are right beside me, waiting for me to turn to you? Help me turn to you more and more, even in so much as a simple lifting of my heart to you, a quick acknowl-

edgement of your presence, or a small smile cast at you. Help me pursue you as zealously as you pursue me, and may I find each moment with you to be the most exhilarating thing in this world. Amen.

11

"Actions Speak Louder Than Words"

Doing What Makes God Happy

"Now by this we may be sure that we know him, if we obey his commandments" (1 John 2:3).

We love to FaceTime with my mom.

Most of the time, the camera points at odd angles, giving her good glimpses of our ceiling fans or tile floor.

Which is how the problem began.

"Is that upside down?" I thought I heard her ask. I couldn't be totally sure as most of the children were jabbering away, excited at the chance to get one iota of attention from the famous Mawmaw. I took a swift glance around the room, looking for anything out of place.

Well, technically, *lots* of things were out of place. And scattered all over our kitchen counters. But none of those things were upside down.

I counted off the children—one, two, three, four—and found that they were all accounted for and, miraculously, all right side up.

Maybe I had misheard. Maybe nothing was upside down.

But then I looked at my son, who was standing by the kitchen sink, and stared with dread at what I knew to be crawling under her skin.

You see, I grew up having a special relationship with my mom. She was a close confidante. My biggest supporter and cheerleader. She was someone I could trust, and thus, she became the person to whom I revealed every detail of my life. Not to mention, she was someone who made me laugh until my sides ached. I look back now and realize that, when given the chance to be with friends or my mom, I often chose my mom because I loved her so much.

Because of all the time we spent together, I know quite a bit about her, too.

Like the fact that she has always liked everything to be in its proper place. Anything even slightly askew thrusts a pointy thorn in her side.

Nothing can be scattered. Everything has to be picked up. Anything on the table has to be parallel at the edges.

Which must have driven her absolutely BONKERS when my brother and I were little, thoughtlessly throwing things all over the place. And then, when we grew up, it must have been even more infuriating. Being the punks we were, my brother and I would intentionally move things out of place and then watch our mother surge into action, righting our wrongs.

So the moment I looked down at my son, I gasped in horror.

There, beneath his feet, the kitchen mat sat upside down, just as my mother suspected. Words like "cappuccino," "mocha," and "java" were flipped on their heads, along with the multicolored coffee mug decorations on its surface.

I sucked in a breath, knowing the intense pain this offense must have caused my poor mother's heart. Who knows how long the mat had egregiously sat there, taunting fellow perfectionists like her? The assault was so blatant that my mom—sweet, detail-oriented lady that she is—picked up on it through a screen while she sat in her own house hundreds of miles away.

It's kind of impressive when you think about it.

"If you think that's bad, you shouldn't come visit," I jokingly said through the phone. "That's the least of our problems over here!"

But later that night, as I stood on the mat washing dishes, I looked at the upside-down coffee mugs beneath my feet, and my mother's words echoed in my mind.

Then, with my bare toes, I flipped the mat around. Not because it bothered me. Clearly it didn't. I hadn't even noticed anything was askew. I turned it right side up solely because I knew it would make my mom happy, and that's all I wanted.

I glanced down at the cups that were now facing me and smiled.

I should show her this, I thought. So I dried my hands on a towel, reached for my phone, and sent her a picture.

Her response, like her approach to life, was perfect. "Thanks," she said and then blew me a kiss through the phone. "I feel much better."

In that moment, I realized that's exactly how I must live as a Christian.

You see, since choosing to follow Jesus, I've grown a special relationship with my Father. He's a close confidante. My biggest supporter and cheerleader. He's someone I can trust, and thus has become the Person to whom I reveal every detail of my life. Not to mention, he's got a pretty wicked sense of humor.

Because of all the time we spend together, I also know quite a bit about how he operates.

Our Father is someone who likes everything to be a certain way. He is perfect, and thus, a perfectionist in the best way. He is perfect love, goodness, joy. Perfect mercy and perfect justice. And he wants that for us, too. Anything less than that (ahem, sin) surely thrusts a pointy thorn in his side, especially since sin isn't merely a harmless, upside-down kitchen mat. Sin is an upside-down heart that wounds both our souls and our relationships with God and others. And God, being the loving Father that he is, wants our good more than anything in the world.

Which means it must drive him absolutely BONKERS when we thoughtlessly throw ourselves at worldly pursuits or other idols, hurting ourselves without even realizing it. And then, when we mature in our faith and keep falling into the same sins, it must be even more infuriating. Being the punks we are, we often *know* what's wrong and choose it anyway.

But no matter how far we've fallen, we can watch our Father surge into action, righting our wrongs if we let him. If we invite him in and rely on his grace for healing and forgiveness.

But it's only through an intimate relationship with God—the *knowing* him, not merely knowing *about* him— that we can understand what pleases him. Then, with his help, we can flip our lives around. Not because what we were doing bothered us. Usually it doesn't (though it probably should). We try to make a change because flipping our hearts right side up makes him happy.

And that's what we truly want.

SNACK TIME!

What "mat" in your life is God inviting you to flip around? Pray for his help and—out of love—work with him to flip it.

PRAYER

Lord, help me be a dutiful daughter who knows you, understands you, and obeys your commands. I turn to you now, Father. Please speak, for I am listening. Even if your voice is filled with agitation, let me hear you. Help me to obey your will, not out of fear, but out of immense love for you. Grow in me a deep desire to please you and grant me the courage to say yes to your call. Amen.

12

"You've Got Your Hands Full"

Pursuing God Like a Little Child

"When you search for me, you will find me; if you
seek me with all your heart" (Jeremiah 29:13).

My oldest daughter's first word was "mama." Before she
really even understood what "mama" meant, she was
saying it. Over and over and over. Then, of course, came
the second word. Ham. (A word that dada was none too
pleased about.)

Over the years, my daughter has packed her vocabulary with a plethora of new words, and yet, "mom" is
still the one she continues to say most. Over and over
and over.

Now, she is the oldest of our children, but all of them
have mastered my short, one-syllable name.

Mom.

They say my name when they need help. They say it
when they're happy, when they're sad, when they're

angry. They say it when they want to show me something or invite me somewhere. Heck, they say it when they don't even mean to sometimes.

Lately, they've even taken to shouting my name to locate me.

Momdar.

That's what I call it, at least. Their ability to find me anywhere—at any time—is impressive, albeit a little smothering.

After some pitter-patter footsteps and a series of distressed "MOOOOM!" shouts, they seem to have no trouble locating me at any given moment. Even if I'm on the toilet.

When I'm desperate (and in need of a shower), I've tried giving them their favorite things. Milk. TV. Graham crackers. But even that doesn't do the trick. Their Momdar is alerted, and sure enough, before the water warms, my youngest toddles into the bathroom to offer me crackers or play on the floor outside the glass door.

As if just being in my presence is better than anything else in this world.

I'm a wanted woman, that's for sure, and these kids are in hot pursuit.

So I've resigned myself to the fact that I'm unlikely to get anything done in private when the kids are awake. Instead, I invite them with me—even to the restroom—and they happily follow.

Always.

It's in those long, dragged-out moments—when my desire for privacy is so palpable it crawls beneath my skin—that I realize God actually *wants* us to seek him this way.

He *wants* us to be in hot pursuit.

He doesn't want one moment of peace and quiet to himself.

He wants all of us, all the time.

Now, after what seems like forever, I have mastered his short, one-syllable name.

God. Christ. Lord.

I say his name when I need help. I say it when I'm happy, when I'm sad, when I'm angry. I say it when I want to show him something or invite him somewhere.

Lately, when I feel all alone in these trenches and so far away from God, I've even taken to shouting his name to locate him.

After a series of distressed "GOOOOD!" shouts, I seem to have no trouble locating him at any given moment.

He's there when I open my Bible.

He's there in the Eucharist at Mass, eagerly waiting for us to receive him.

He's there, sitting majestically in the monstrance at Adoration.

Heck, he's even there when I'm utterly exhausted, driving through the grocery store parking lot, and a spot in the front row miraculously opens up.

Because, in reality, he loves us so much, he's never far away. He doesn't want to do anything privately. Instead, he wants us to go with him. Everywhere. All the time.

Sometimes he'll invite us somewhere exotic and beautiful. Fun, even. Other times he'll invite us to some pretty filthy places. But no matter what, he'll be there, too.

And I want to be a child who happily follows.

Always.

SNACK TIME!

Seek God by calling his name.

PRAYER

God, help me to follow you wherever you go. Like a child, I am unable to care for myself and others unless I have your help. Develop in me a burning love for you and inspire me to follow you everywhere. If I ever find myself alone and don't know where you are, help me to call out to you, for your name alone has power. May I run to you and pursue you zealously, as you also pursue me. May I do nothing apart from you. When I tend to the needs of my family, be with me. In my work, be with me. In my rest and relaxation, be with me. In all that I say and do, Lord, be with me. I ask this in your most holy name. Amen.

13

"Because I Said So"

Trusting God

"For as the heavens are higher than the earth,
 so are my ways higher than your ways
 and my thoughts than your thoughts" (Isaiah 55:9).

The first time I laid eyes on my daughter, she looked like a pea pod. She had only existed for six weeks inside my womb, and yet there she was, dangling from my uterine wall by her head. A vegetable-shaped person with a swooshing heartbeat.

Since then, she has grown. Morphed, really. I mean now, at three years old, at least she looks human. That's progress.

Also, at three years old, she has talents and preferences. Strengths and weaknesses. And a ridiculously insatiable curiosity. There are some days I wonder if she's forgotten every word in her growing vocabulary aside from one: "Why?"

"Baby, eat your dinner."

"Why?"

"Because food gives you energy and makes you strong."

"Why?"

I can't explain carbs and lipids and proteins to a toddler, so I simply shrug. "That's just how it is."

"Why?"

Every single conversation goes this way. Life constantly gets boiled down to the molecular level and I'm expected to explain that to a three-year-old.

For a while, I was tempted to bypass the spiraling conversations and reply with an age-old line:

Because I said so.

But the apple doesn't fall far from the tree, and I immediately asked myself, "Why? Why would I say so?"

For the most part, I discovered, I said so because I truly believe that my decisions are what's best for my daughter. The tricky part was to help her understand that and trust it.

So I decided that the next time she asked her new favorite question, I would explain what "because I said so" really means.

It's actually a question: "Do you trust me?"

She soon gave me the opportunity.

"Baby, it's bedtime," I said when she came out of her room late one night. "You need to stay in your bed and go to sleep."

"Why?" she whined.

"Do you know that I want what's best for you?" I asked.

Her little face looked up at me, partly confused, partly shocked.

"My decisions are good for you, even if they're not what you want," I explained further, brushing blond hair behind her tiny ear. "My job as your mom is to keep you healthy and strong, so my decisions are meant to keep you healthy and strong."

Contempt scrunched her face and wrinkled her miniature nose.

"Do you trust me?" I asked.

She paused for a moment to take in my words. "Yes," she finally muttered.

"And right now, going to sleep is what's best for you. Do you trust me?"

"Okay." She huffed her displeasure but marched back to her room and curled up on the bed, ready for sleep.

* * *

Now, six weeks into my third pregnancy, I sit half-naked on a doctor's table because the bleeding hasn't stopped for four days. The doctor lumbers in, draped in his white coat and a thick cloak of concern.

"This doesn't look normal," he says slowly, pointing out all the abnormalities on the ultrasound. Highlighting all the shades of gray on his black-and-white screen.

There's no swooshing heartbeat, as there had been with my daughter. No sign of life in the mass inside me. In fact, we can't see a mass inside me at all. No baby in my womb. Did the baby die before it was big enough to be visible on the ultrasound?

The doctor doesn't need to speak. His drooping eyes and deliberate demeanor say it all, but he keeps talking anyway. I can practically see him hand-select each word before it comes out of his mouth.

"I expect this pregnancy will miscarry," he says. "I suggest we vacuum everything out of the uterus."

The world around me spins too quickly. "I'm sorry, what?"

The doctor's droll voice begins to answer my question. He may have said something about genetic abnormalities and that we did nothing wrong, but I don't really hear. I'm too busy grappling with the diagnosis.

Miscarry.

From a distance, the word seems innocent enough. Commonplace. Easy, even.

But when you get closer, it reeks of blood. Like iron and death.

And when you get a little too close, it sounds like pain. The pain of childbirth. The pain of a lost child.

Miscarry.

What the heck? Why is this happening?

This time I ask the questions quietly, in the space where only God will hear.

I can almost feel him kneel beside me in this sterile room and tuck my hair behind my ear. Can nearly feel his life-giving breath on my face, despite the death in my womb. I can almost hear the question that will determine everything.

"Do you trust me?"

SNACK TIME!

What can you trust God with right now?

PRAYER

God, you know the difficulties I face and how I struggle. I don't know why you've handed me this cross, but I will carry it with all my might because it was a gift from you. Help me remember that your ways are always better than mine and relieve me of the urge to control or fix things on my own. I praise you and thank you for being a God who transforms death into life, loss into hope. I offer you all my pain. Turn these tears into holy water and my suffering into salvation. Amen.

14

"Through Thick and Thin"

God Is Always Working for Our Good

"We know that all things work together for good for those who love God, who are called according to his purpose" (Romans 8:28).

I met my third baby one day after everything had been surgically sucked out of me.

Not in the remains from the surgery. Not even in a photograph of the carnage.

But *inside* my body. On an ultrasound of my Fallopian tube.

There, nestled in the nook of a narrow tube, I saw her. Or him. Whatever the gender, the baby was clearly still growing inside me. Which, ironically, was the problem. Its body kept growing—kept *living*—inside my Fallopian tube, stretching and pressing against the delicate tunnel.

And the tube was on the verge of rupture.

"We need to perform another surgery." My doctor could hardly believe what he was saying. *I* could hardly believe what he was saying. Hadn't they just performed surgery on me the day before? The one that emptied everything from my uterus? Wasn't that supposed to fix everything?

Wrinkles deepened in my doctor's forehead. "And we need to do the surgery today."

I nodded, unable to peel my eyes off this bean-shaped treasure. I thought I'd already said goodbye to this baby. This baby who, apparently, was still alive.

The little black peanut looked so innocent, cuddled up cozily in the tiny tube where only 1–2 percent of pregnancies occur. If only it had traveled an inch or so farther . . .

In that moment, there was nothing I wanted more than that baby. To learn the sound of his laughter or discover her greatest passion. To reach out and touch it, even if my fingers only grazed a glass screen.

There was nothing I wanted more than to prove to this baby that I could be a good mother.

But that option didn't exist.

"Tubal pregnancies are very dangerous." An added layer of seriousness darkened the doctor's voice. "If we don't perform surgery and your tube ruptures, you could die from internal bleeding. If we do the surgery, I'll most likely have to take the Fallopian tube."

I nodded again, like I was consenting. Like I had consented to any of this.

Then, after bursting through the front doors of the doctor's office, I sank onto the curb with my husband where the Texas summer clung to me like my diagnosis. Hot. Sticky. Nauseating.

"Do you trust me?" God asked, the same way he did when we first received the misdiagnosis of miscarriage.

I couldn't think, let alone trust. Trusting something —even God—felt risky now. Naive. On the verge of irresponsible.

So I pushed him away.

I could only do what I'd been instructed to do. And right then, I was being instructed to have another surgery. So I signed the papers and agreed to lose my baby— again—along with half of my future fertility.

* * *

When I woke up, the drugs were strong. I didn't know where I was or who was beside me. All I knew was that I was shivering away the anesthesia and each twitch set my stomach on fire.

Finally, I saw his face. My husband. My best friend. The captain of our marriage.

"The doctor said everything went fine. Your Fallopian tube *was* ruptured. Apparently, it had also twisted up and attached to your abdomen wall." He gently touched my hand, making sure to avoid the IV needle and tubes shooting out of my arms like wild veins. "Doc said that saved you."

For a moment, the drugs stopped tugging at my eyelids. Even the shivers stopped.

"Do you trust me?" God asked for the umpteenth time since this all began.

This time, I heard him through the madness and finally granted him an answer. Finally allowed him to stay.

Funny how his tone never wavers. Never condescends. Never says, "I told you so." He doesn't force me to trust him or state it as a command. He simply asks.

Do you trust me?

Because the truth is—whether I trusted him or not—he's been on my team the whole time. Long before I knew I needed a teammate, he was there.

Before I knew anything needed to be fixed, God knew.

And he chose to fix it. He chose to save me.

I imagine him flawlessly twisting my Fallopian tube and attaching it securely to my abdominal membranes. Tying the delicate tube into a knot that would stop the blood. Creating the perfect tourniquet before the injury even took place.

But this isn't the first time God's done that for me.

Long before I knew I needed a teammate, he was there, willingly hanging on a cross. His own blood gushing from his body with no tourniquet to stop it.

Before I knew anything needed to be fixed, God knew.

And he chose to fix it. He chose to save me.

SNACK TIME!

Ask God to help you trust him with those areas in your life that seem scary, overwhelming, or confusing.

PRAYER

Jesus, I trust in you, but sometimes it's hard. Help me trust in you, even when I cannot see. Even when I feel like I'm drowning. Remind me of your saving grace and give me the patience to wait for you, trusting that in your timing you will rescue me. Until that glorious moment, grant that I may use these difficult times as an offering to you. Lord, it is through difficulties that saints are made. Transform me now, through the gift of my sufferings, into a great saint, that I may show you patience in adversity and faith in uncertainty. For you alone, Lord, have the words of everlasting life. To whom else would I go? To whom else could I possibly give my yes? You are the only one who deserves it. Give me the strength to say yes to you, even when the road is difficult and marked with suffering. Amen.

15

"Blessing in Disguise"

God Can See What We Can't

"For surely I know the plans I have for you, says the Lord, plans for your welfare and not for harm, to give you a future with hope" (Jeremiah 29:11).

My kids always seem to know what they want.

Milk. Snacks. A blanket. Socks. More snacks.

And that's just at bedtime.

They're pros at wanting stuff.

Take it from my son. He was only eight months old and couldn't even speak yet, but he had the gift of knowing what he wanted and communicating it clearly. (If you don't believe me, you should have seen what happened when Mom walked out of the room.)

At that stage, everything became tricky. Loading and unloading the dishwasher became an all-out war. One day, he army-crawled into the kitchen and climbed straight into the dishwasher (literally, *into* the dishwasher). I snatched him out and plopped him back on the floor, but he had found the fully stocked armory. Before I could stop him, he grabbed the sharpest, most serrated knife on the bottom shelf, and I wrestled it out of his tiny, dimple-knuckled fingers before he could do any damage. Sweating, I raced to remove the remaining sharp knives and breakable dishes and put them out of his reach. Finally, at the sight of an empty dishwasher, I breathed a sigh of relief.

It seemed the battle was over, and the baby crawled along on his merry little way.

Directly into the open cabinet filled with Tupperware.

He reached for the biggest, glassiest baking dish, and the moment his little fingers seized the smooth, clear glass, I pulled him away and closed the cabinet door.

Oooh, he did *not* like that.

He sat and sobbed. He kicked and screamed. He tried to fight me and pry the door back open when he thought I wasn't looking.

All he could see was the shiny thing that had been right in front of him. It had been within reach. He'd had it in his hands, for goodness' sake. And then, *poof*, the shiny thing was gone.

The kid didn't know what a baking dish was—heck, he didn't even know what *glass* was. He had no idea what danger and destruction could have come from playing with sharp knives or glass bakeware.

All he knew was that he wanted them.

Yet, as his mom, I closed those doors for him out of love.

I imagine that if I hadn't, my son would have learned that knives and broken glass can slice through flesh. He would have learned a lot about blood and pain and stitches and scars. And, perhaps, he might have learned a fearful aversion to the dishwasher and cookware.

But there was no way he could have known any of that.

Heck, even as an adult, I act the same way.

I'm a pro at wanting stuff.

I always seem to think I know exactly what I want.

A spouse. A car. A baby. A house. A promotion. A bigger house.

And, because I'm a big nerd, I dream of writing and publishing lots of books.

Which is probably why the first time I got a positive pregnancy test, I fell to the floor. With trembling hands, I pulled myself back to my feet, unsure how to tell my husband the news. We were newlyweds. We were clueless. And we were flat broke.

At that time, I had just started a career in journalism. I loved the writing. The deadlines and quick turnarounds. The extra income. But that day in the bathroom, as I stared at the word PREGNANT, I could feel God pulling me away and closing that door. We had no family nearby. No help. We couldn't afford child care. How could I host interviews while holding a new-born? How could I continue to travel and meet the people I was writing about? How could I manage to hit deadlines while spending all day and all-night tending to the needs of a new person? Knowing me—tunnel-visioned, Type-A, perfectionistic me—I couldn't do it. Someone else might have been able to juggle those things, but not me. I would grind myself straight into the grave.

So the door to journalism started to slowly close before my eyes.

Ooooh, I did *not* like that.

I sat and sobbed. I kicked and screamed. I tried to fight God and pry the door back open when I thought he wasn't looking.

All I could see was the shiny thing that had been right in front of me. It had been within reach. I'd had it in my hands, for goodness' sake. And then, *poof,* the shiny thing was gone.

I didn't know much about a long-term journalism career. All I knew was that I wanted it.

Yet my Father closed that door out of love.

But how could I have understood that by pulling me away from that thing I loved, God was actually helping me? How could I have anticipated the joy that explodes inside me when my daughter smiles at me or wraps her arms around my torso? How could I have ever dreamed of the wonderful, caring girl she would become? How could I have comprehended how much the world—and our family—would need her? And how could I possibly have known that God was hand-delivering an opportunity to use my passion for words to write about faith and motherhood?

I couldn't.

But God promises that his plans are always for my good. His plans won't hurt me. His plans won't shatter. His plans will always give me a hope and a future.

And *that* is worth pursuing.

SNACK TIME!

How might the closed doors in your life be a loving gift?

PRAYER

Jesus, I place my desires at your feet and ask you for them now. Yet, not my will, but yours be done. Let me learn from you, Lord, who in the Garden of Gethsemane placed your requests before the Father but were also faithful enough to choose his will over your own. You willingly accepted the crucifixion because it was your Father's will. Give me the grace and strength to model my heart after your Sacred Heart. Remind me that your will for my life is not only in the future, but in this moment. Help me live out what you have for me today with faith, joy, and love. Amen.

16

"Live and Learn"

When It Feels Like You're Suffocating

"Your kingdom come.
Your will be done,
        on earth as it is in heaven" (Matthew 6:10).

When my son was two, we got a refrigerator with a freezer on the bottom, which didn't seem like a big deal.

Until my son discovered popsicles.

One night before dinner, he wrapped his little fingers around the thick handle and tugged. Hard. But nothing happened. He knew his muscles weren't strong enough to open the big door, but he's headstrong enough to keep trying. (He gets that from his momma.)

So he tugged and tugged, yanking at a door that he had neither the strength nor the authority to open, until desperation and hunger were at their angriest. Waves of sobs racked his little body and choked his breathing. Only then did he turn to me. The lady with the clearance to open 'er up.

"Popsicle!" he cried, jimmying the handle.

"It's almost time for dinner," I said, stirring a pot of boiling noodles. "We can have popsicles tomorrow."

"NO DINNER! NO 'MORROW!!!!!!" He turned back to the freezer and panic consumed his face. His breath accelerated and hiccupped. Previously held-back tears flooded his flushed cheeks. A popsicle—his *happiness*—was right on the other side of that door.

"POPSIIIIIIIIICLLLLE!!!!!!!!!!" He thrashed desperately, hyperventilating, pounding away at the door as though his life depended on it.

"I'm making spaghetti," I said calmly, hoping my voice could ring louder than his maniacal screaming. "Would you like to help me?"

If he heard me, he didn't show it. He was too focused on his lack of oxygen, too busy tugging hysterically at a locked door. Surely that cold, juicy popsicle came packaged with the giant life-giving breath he needed to survive this torment. Right? "Open dis!"

"No popsicles right now, bud, but you can go play with your fire trucks."

Spaghetti. Fire trucks. Two of his favorite things in the entire world.

But they weren't enough.

So I offered him other things he loves.

Books?

"NO!"

Sisters?

"NOOOO!"

My hugs?

"NOOOOO! OPEN DIIIIIIISSSSS!!!!"

He slinked to the ground, exhausted. Defeated. Succumbing to the suffocation that came from not getting what he wanted.

"Popsicle," he whimpered, mostly to himself.

His little heart was set on an appetizer. One that would mostly melt down his arm before he could even taste the goodness. One that, unbeknownst to him, would leave him hungry.

All the while, I was right beside him preparing a full-on feast. One that would nourish and strengthen him. One from which he could get his complete fill. One that would take away those feelings of hunger and longing and replace them with strength and joy. But he couldn't tear his gaze from the closed door, the one that seemingly promised all that his heart desired.

As I stood there, watching him wallow in self-pity and sorrow, it occurred to me that he gets that from his momma, too.

How many times have I tried to bust down a door, convinced that what lay behind it promised happiness and fulfillment? How many times have I been suffocated by the constant demands of motherhood and dreamed of having something else—*anything* else—just so I could breathe for a second?

Without even asking my Father, I've walked right up

to locked doors and tugged. Hard. Of course nothing happened. I knew my muscles weren't strong enough to open them. But that wouldn't stop me from trying.

So I tugged and tugged, yanking at doors that I had neither the strength nor the authority to open, until desperation and longing were at their angriest. Only then did I think to turn to my Father. The One with the clearance to open 'er up.

"Open this, God!" I commanded, jimmying the handle.

"It's time for something else," he said.

"NO SOMETHING ELSE!!!!!!" I turned face-to-face with my chosen door. Previously held-back tears flooded my flushed cheeks. Why did it . . . feel . . . like I . . . couldn't . . . breathe? Waves of panic racked my body. Motherhood was too much, too constant. I had to get away for a second. Had to find air.

Publication for my writing. Adult conversation. A minute of peace and quiet to myself for once. I wanted them. Needed them. Couldn't breathe without them. But every single one of those things was just on the other side of that door. Unreachable. So I thrashed desperately, pounding away at the door as though my life depended on it.

"I have other plans for you. They'll help you, not hurt you," God said calmly, hoping his voice could ring louder than my maniacal screaming. "Would you like to help me?"

If I heard him, I didn't show it. I was too focused on my lack of oxygen, too busy tugging hysterically at a locked door. Surely, the other side came packaged with the giant life-giving breath I needed to survive this suffocation. Right?

"You can't have those things right now, but you can go exercise or have a cup of coffee."

Exercise. Coffee. Two of my favorite things in the entire world.

But they weren't enough.

So he offered me other things I love.

Food?

"NO!"

A bed to sleep in?

"NOOOO!"

His love?

"NOOOOO! OPEN THIIIIIIIISSSSS!!!!"

I slinked to the ground, exhausted. Defeated. Succumbing to the suffocation of raising little kids.

My heart was set on an appetizer. One that would mostly melt before I could taste the goodness. One that, unbeknownst to me, would eventually leave me hungry.

All the while, God was right beside me, preparing a full-on feast. One that would nourish and strengthen me. One from which I could get my complete fill. One that would take away those feelings of hunger and suffocation and replace them with strength and joy.

It wasn't until I tore my gaze from the closed door that I realized that the Source of joy and fulfillment was on *this* side. With me. He was within arm's reach, not locked behind some sealed door. *He* was the freedom I craved—my Breath of Life.

I already had everything I needed. Everything I wanted. All at once, my prayer changed.

"Close that door, God," I pleaded. "Open *me*."

SNACK TIME!

When you feel like you're suffocating, tear your gaze from the closed doors in your life and lock eyes with God.

PRAYER

Lord, sometimes I can get tunnel-visioned on what I think I want. I assume that whatever that thing is, it will bring me happiness. I believe it will give me the breath I need when I feel suffocated in these trenches. Remind me, O Breath of God, that you are the only One who can do that. Breathe into me as you once did into Adam, that I may become fully alive in you. Then let me walk with you, hand in hand, as together we set forth on the journey you have prepared for me. Amen.

PART III

Who Are You?

17

"You'll Live"

Nothing Can Separate You from God's Love

"For I am convinced that neither death, nor life, nor angels, nor rulers, nor things present, nor things to come, nor powers, nor height, nor depth, nor anything else in all creation, will be able to separate us from the love of God in Christ Jesus our Lord" (Romans 8:38–39).

My kids have been passing around the flu like a game of hot, hot, feverish potato.

So far, my two-year-old has been hit the worst.

For nearly a week now, his favorite words have been "uh-oh" and "throw up." The stomach bug completely stripped him of his smiley, independent demeanor and replaced it with whining, screaming, hitting, and the inability to ever be put down.

So I've carried him around day after day, listening to his tantrums, absorbing his fever, and knowing that at any moment he could hurl all over me.

I've spent every waking moment with the kid, and even found myself waking up in the middle of the night just to think about him—about how utterly exhausting he has been lately.

And then I remembered the story of his birth.

How his heart rate decelerated every two minutes with each of my contractions. How a stampede of nurses rushed to my room each time that happened to pump me with fluids or readjust my limp, bloated, epidural-filled body. How that made for a *really* long twenty hours of labor. How, when his heart rate dropped dangerously low, the doctor finally had to cut him from my body with an emergency C-section.

There I was, lying on an operating table, in a deluge of my blood, too weak and scared to move as they refilled me with my own organs.

The kid and I had been through the gamut together, and it nearly killed us both.

The poor baby's face was splotched purple with bruising—the swelling so bad he couldn't even open his eyes—and his skull squished to the side like a squashed melon.

But it was official.

I had delivered him. He was alive.

My son's birth was by far the most traumatic and dramatic of all my children's births. At the time, we didn't know if he would live. At some points, I wasn't even sure that *I* would live. So when the doctor finally pulled him through the incision in my stomach, I half-expected to hear nothing but dead silence.

And, for a moment, that's exactly what happened.

Then that baby's sweet voice entered the world. Not in a loud scream, but in a tiny whimper. One that made my heart trip over itself and rejoice and reach for him all the more.

After the nurses examined him to make sure there was no heart or brain damage, they finally, *finally* put him on my chest. For the life of me, nothing could have taken that sweet boy out of my arms.

The story of his birth—the tumultuous journey of what it took to get him here—now bonds us forever. So strongly, in fact, that nothing—not even terrible, trying, sick-kid behavior—can strip me of my love for him.

All the difficulties, the strife, the *exhaustion* as of late faded to the back of my mind, buried beneath thick layers of love and the memories of what it took to get him here.

But Lord knows *I'm* sick, too. And my condition is both chronic and potentially terminal. This sickness—this *sin*—completely stripped me of my pure and holy demeanor and replaced it with whining and selfishness.

That's when I remembered the story of *my* birth.

My spiritual birth, that is.

How the Son's Sacred Heart must have dropped when his own people demanded his execution. How a stampede of Roman soldiers rushed in to bludgeon him and shove his weak, swollen, bloody body toward the cross and then nail him to it.

How that made for a *really* long Friday.

There he was, hanging from a cross, in a deluge of his blood, as they pierced his side, completing my birth.

He had been through the gamut for me, and it actually killed him.

His face was disfigured with sweat and blood, dust, and spit—flesh ripped and dangling from his body—and his skull was pierced with the long points of mocking thorns.

But it was official.

He had delivered me. I would live.

As agonizing as my labor was, the cross was way worse. Yet Jesus still chose to go through it. For me. For you. For your children and mine. For the entire Church born from his pierced side that day on Calvary. So that none of us would have to endure the same agony or the even worse pain of being eternally separated from God.

The story of our birth to eternal life—the tumultuous journey of what it took to get us here—now bonds us with him forever. So strongly, in fact, that nothing—neither death nor life, nor angels, nor principalities, nor things present, nor things to come, nor powers—can strip him of his love for us.

And all the difficulties, the strife, the *exhaustion* that we cause him fade to the back of his mind, buried beneath thick layers of love and the memories of what it took to get us here.

SNACK TIME!

When my son was born, his voice was the sweetest sound I'd ever heard. Our Heavenly Father feels the same way about you. Take some time right now to use your voice to talk to him.

PRAYER

In dying on the cross, you brought me to life. How can it be that you endured such agony—such shame—for me? How could I possibly deserve such a favor? It's impossible to deserve, let alone earn, what you give so freely. I pray that I may live my whole life as a song of praise and thanks to you. Give me a heart filled with unshakable faith in the One who delivered me—a heart that will trip over itself and rejoice and reach for you always. Amen.

18

"Could You Lend Me a Hand?"

What Asking for Help Really Means

"Love one another with mutual affection; outdo one another in showing honor" (Romans 12:10).

I grew up thinking I had to do everything myself. That I was only worth as much as I could accomplish. And if I couldn't do something, well . . . then I wasn't as valuable.

My perfectionist heart hated that idea. I had to be perfect, had to be the best. At everything.

So, I never *ever* asked for help. From anyone. It'd be a burden on them and a sign of weakness in me. A black mark on the squeaky-clean record I worked so hard to maintain.

After all, wasn't help just something people did out of obligation? Something they secretly hated to do, huffing behind your back and resenting you for inconveniencing them?

It made me shudder to think about it.

No, nothing good came from asking for help.

With this mindset, I ground through life—through sports, school, relationships, *everything*—with my head down, bulldozing my path one day at a time, determined to be valuable. To be favored. To be unresented.

All the while, God must've been laughing. He knew what was in store for me. He knew what he'd done.

He, in his infinite wisdom and creativity (and wicked sense of humor), had created the perfect boy for me. One who not only checked all the boxes of what I dreamed of in a husband, but surpassed them. A man unlike any I'd ever met before.

A man who—along with his many other beautiful qualities—had a heart that thrived on acts of service.

Ugh.

Every time we approached his car, he intentionally locked the doors—forcing me to wait, anxiety churning in my stomach, as he swung around and opened the passenger door for me.

He made surprise trips across the country, driving sixteen hours in a stiff company van, just to visit me—a feat I welcomed with a disheartened high five.

He cooked elaborate dinners for the two of us, and each time, I cringed at how much work he had undertaken on my behalf.

Dating him was difficult.

Not because I didn't like him. No, this handsome boy had completely stolen my heart the first moment I laid eyes on him. It was precisely *because* my heart was his—because I knew I wanted to be with him forever—that I writhed at all his servitude. Wouldn't he get burned out serving me all the time? Wouldn't he start resenting me? Wouldn't he start seeing me as some incapable, dependent weight that held him down?

"You don't have to do all this for me, you know," I said one night, asserting my capability, my competence—my *worth*—through a mouthful of his homemade oatmeal chocolate chip cookies. They were delicious, but they were also saturated with unnecessary labor. Labor he had undertaken for *me*. It had to stop, and it had to stop now. "I don't like it when people do things for me. I can do all this stuff by myself, especially open doors."

He furrowed his brows in total confusion. "I *like* doing things for you," he said. "I know you can open doors, but when you let me do it for you, *you* show *me* love. You let me do something I like to do."

My head jerked as though I'd been slapped. "What?" I asked, my mind whirling, trying to process what he'd just said. I glanced down at the cookie in my hand. He actually *liked* baking these? It was *loving* to let him serve me? I shook my head in disbelief. That couldn't be right. I must've misheard him.

As though sensing my thoughts, he continued. "When you let me serve you, you give me a chance to be more like Jesus."

In that moment, decades' worth of lies shattered inside me. In their place, the truth blossomed.

I smiled at this newfound discovery. Asking for help was loving. It gave people a chance to be Christ-like.

I've carried that with me, joyfully letting him open doors and cook breakfasts and do whatever needs to be done. I serve him in return, trying to anticipate his needs and fill them before he can, as we playfully compete to see who can serve the other better.

Because of how freely he serves, I'm much better loved than ever before. And, because of his selflessness, I have learned how to love better than ever before. Now, I find that I'm happy to cook dinners and wash dishes and fold laundry. There's no resentment. No obligation. Just a playful desire to beat him to the punch.

Yet now, as a mother, I witness the mind-boggling phenomenon of genetics at work. My two-year-old has discovered that she can do things. On her own. And, by golly, she wants to do *everything* that way. Just like her momma. Heaven help her.

"BY MYSELF!" she shouts, echoing my former favorite words as she struggles to zip a zipper or put on shoes or . . . do just about anything.

"Okay," I say, kneeling beside her, praying that a bit of my husband is also nestled in her heart. "If you need help, just ask."

She jimmies the stubborn zipper a few more times, then looks to me. "Help, please, Mommy."

"I'd be happy to help you." I smile, grateful she's catching on much sooner than I did. "Helping you gives me a chance to be more like Jesus."

SNACK TIME!

We're not meant to do everything by ourselves. Even Jesus needed Simon of Cyrene to help him carry his cross. Is there one thing you could ask someone for help with today?

PRAYER

Jesus, you are the Way, the Truth, and the Life. When we hear your Truth and walk in your Way, we find true Life, and we find it in abundance. Just before the Passover, when you knew the Passion was looming, you chose to wash your apostles' dirty feet. You were constantly serving, constantly giving. But you also allowed your friend Mary to anoint your feet as a sign of her love for you. Lord Jesus, help us to be like you—sometimes being the one who washes the feet, but at other times, being humble enough to give another the chance to wash ours. Amen.

19

"Birds of a Feather Flock Together"

Be Who You Really Are

"Celebrate and rejoice, because this brother of yours was dead and has come to life; he was lost and has been found" (Luke 15:32).

My son has disappeared.

Not physically, thank heavens.

But my smiley, go-with-the-flow, happy-to-help toddler has been replaced by some body snatcher who constantly sulks, shoulders drooped, head down, shouting things like, "I don't want to!" or some whiny form of "Stooooop!"

It's exhausting.

Mass has become difficult. Nap time is impossible. Getting him to eat a meal? Forget about it. Simply playing together is now a challenge.

But we still grind through all those things because we know who he is—who he really is—and, by golly, we love him.

So it wasn't much of a surprise when his legs went limp in the parking lot as we walked into Mass. Then he planted his sneakers firmly on the sidewalk, refusing to move another step.

"Come on, bud," I called.

He crossed his arms over his chest and huffed.

I steeled myself for battle, then scooped him off the ground and carried him inside.

"That's not who you are," I reminded him, as I do several times every day. "You are good. You are kind. You are sweet."

I went on and on, detailing the person I know he is.

You are loving. You are helpful. You are a good listener. You are smart. You are silly. You like to make people laugh.

He relaxed in my arms and rested his head against my shoulder as I carried him inside. My heart melted.

There's my boy.

Together, as a family, we processed down the aisle, genuflected to say hi to Jesus, and slid into the front pew.

Then I made a fatal mistake: I whispered my son's name in his ear.

But the boy in my lap was not my son. At least, not at the moment.

"Don't talk to me, Mom!" he said in a volume that was definitely *not* our Mass voice. He pushed himself off my lap, scampered away, and then sat, hunched, legs draped over the side of the pew. As far away from the rest of us as possible.

If he were my first child—heck, maybe even my second—I would have hunted him down and forced him into my lap like a normal child SO HELP ME.

But he's the third. And his two older sisters both went through this and turned out just fine. (I think.)

This, I've learned, is a developmental stage that his two-year-old brain simply cannot avoid.

And this, I've also learned, is not who he is.

He's not the gargoyle at the end of the pew.

He's the boy who laughs so hard he snorts. The boy who pretends to be an altar server and dreams of one day becoming a basketball player. The boy whose face lights up when he runs to me first thing in the morning. And, when I scoop him into my arms, he's the boy who gently rubs my back and says, "Mommy, you're a great mommy."

At some point, that boy will return. It might not be today. It might not be tomorrow. It might not be until after his next birthday, when these twos stop being so terrible. But at some point, he will be himself again.

How do I know?

Because he's mine.

I've been here with him since the moment he existed. Who else would know him better than I do?

I know who he really is, who he was created to be.

I glanced his way a few times during Mass, but the boy didn't move a muscle.

So I left him there. Alone. Sad. Separated.

He didn't need a consequence from me. He was inflicting isolation—the most painful consequence—on himself.

Finally, somewhere near the end, he looked my way. I opened my arms, inviting him to come back, and he willingly ran to me and snuggled into my lap.

As the final hymn played, he danced at my feet and shouted goodbye as the priest processed away. My heart swelled with love for him.

There's my boy.

At that moment, though, I thought of all the times I've been moody and self-absorbed. All the pity parties I've thrown for myself. All the times I've held God at arms' length or ignored him altogether.

And how that must really drive God nuts. Because, I've learned, that is not who I am.

I'm the girl who dreams of living in a way that shows everyone how valuable and loved they are. The girl whose face lights up when she gets to sit on the porch with a cup of coffee and her Bible first thing in the morning. And, when I encounter God, I'm the girl who, with great awe, says, "Wow, you're a really great Father."

And no matter what, that girl will always return.

How do I know?

Because I'm his.

He's been with me since the moment I existed. Who else would know me better than he does?

He knows who I really am, who he created me to be.

And he whispers it into my ear if I listen closely enough.

You are good. You are fearfully and wonderfully made. You do not have a spirit of cowardice, but rather a spirit of power and of love and of self-discipline.

Patiently, he waits for me to turn to him, to *choose* him.

To be who I really am.

SNACK TIME!

Choose God and run back to him.

PRAYER

God, thank you for creating me the way you did. Help me to see myself the way you do—valuable and beloved just the way I am. Inspire and teach me to live in a way that serves and pleases you, Lord. I run to you now with abandon. I choose you. I choose to be the person you dreamt of when you pieced me together. Grant that I may have the strength to resist the things of this world that turn me sour. Instead, keep my eyes fixed on you, pressing forward toward the prize that you have won for me. Amen.

20

"Someday You'll Have One Just Like You"

Being God's Reflection

"Then God said, 'Let us make humankind in our image, according to our likeness'" (Genesis 1:26).

It's been exactly one year since I first saw my face on someone else.

From the beginning, I could easily spot her and claim her as my own. And throughout the 365 days that have passed, the similarities have only grown stronger.

The girl with big eyes and board-straight hair. The girl with a constant smile and audible gasps over balls, books, and airplanes. The girl who sticks out her tongue in stern concentration and also downright silliness.

My daughter, my mini-me.

It's peculiar, this phenomenon. This ability to see yourself in something that lives and breathes outside of you. In something that reflects you perfectly but is not your reflection.

This opportunity must be rare, I think. Not only do the stars and planets have to align just right, but so do the egg, sperm, and impending chromosomes.

And I'm so glad I got to have a mini-me.

As I sit, gazing at the miniature version of myself, I wonder if this is how God must feel. Has he looked at me and relished all the ways I reflect him? Even more so, has he gazed at all of creation—the hundreds of billions of people who have existed in the world throughout history—and thought the same thing?

Though we look at each other and find such vast differences, surely he sees each individual and marvels at their striking similarity to their Father. I imagine he's been doing this since the start of humanity. Over and over. Billions and billions of times.

And we still haven't completely captured him. (Well, other than Jesus.)

Surely, God sees his reflection in my husband's self-sacrificial heart. He must catch a glimpse of himself in the joy and sense of humor of each of my children. He's there in my parents' and in-laws' generosity. In a friend's inspiring faithfulness and trust. In another's encouragement. In another's empathy. And in yet another's mercy and unconditional love.

God glances around and sees bits of himself everywhere. So much so, we can be sure that even strangers resemble him in some way. He placed us all around the earth, like billions of pieces in a gigantic jigsaw puzzle, so we could get a bigger, clearer picture of who he is.

My hope is that from the beginning of time, God could easily spot me and claim me as his own. That throughout the days that pass, the similarities only grow stronger.

That on the day I meet him face-to-face, he'll gaze upon me with love. "My daughter," he'll say. "I'm so glad I got to have a mini-me."

SNACK TIME!

Keep an eye out for the way people (including you!) reflect God. Thank those people for giving you a glimpse of God through their actions and personalities.

PRAYER

God, thank you for being who you are—a God worthy of worship. A God so close and relatable but also altogether inexhaustible. A God who, throughout millennia, never has been and never will be fully grasped. Give me a glimpse of your holy face, that I may know you better. As a baby examines the face of the one who holds her, so I long to examine you, Father. Holy Spirit, give me the gift of knowledge and understanding, that I may know you better and thus reflect you more clearly. Help me to recognize you in myself and in others. Lord Jesus, transform me into a living monstrance, so that when others look upon me, they will see you. Amen.

21

"If Your Friends Jumped Off a Bridge, Would You?"

Who Do You Imitate?

"Be imitators of me, as I am of Christ" (1 Corinthians 11:1).

I'm convinced my daughters are lizards. Chameleons, to be exact. They—along with all other kids their age— have an uncanny ability to transform into anyone they've been near.

My kids see everything that other kids do, then they want to *do* everything other kids do.

It's disturbing to watch your own flesh and blood become someone else.

Just the other day, my four-year-old strapped herself into her car seat and began to morph into a girl she'd been spending time with recently.

She crossed her arms over her chest, scrunched her nose, and huffed. "I'm hungry. I want to eat."

If I hadn't been looking, I might have thought that my daughter's friend had sneaked into our car. The mannerisms were that spot on. Even my daughter's voice changed to copy this other girl.

It was terrifying.

And downright infuriating.

In my most dire attempt to stay patient, I closed my eyes and sighed. "Baby, I love you most when you're most like yourself."

"What do you mean?" Her pouty face stared at me from the backseat.

I know my daughter in her truest form. She's a girl who earns special treats for being kind, and then waits at the end of an imaginary line while insisting her invisible friends get the goodies first. She's a girl who gives toys to babies and tickles their toes just to make them smile. She's a girl who loves people greatly.

But in that moment, her future flooded my mind: school, sports, dreams, boys, jobs, perhaps a family of her own.

How different would she be at the end of her journey? Would the girl I know fade away over time?

I glanced back into her little face—the one she had finally stopped scrunching—and my heart ached. It begged for my daughter to cherish and protect who she is at her core, the way I do. But it'd be impossible to explain all that to a four-year-old.

"God made you to be you. When you become like someone else, *you* disappear." I exhaled and shrugged. "Please don't disappear."

But, I realized, I too am a chameleon. We all are. We see everything in the world, and then we want to *do* all those things. *Be* all those things.

And I bet it's disturbing for our Father to watch his children mimic someone else. Especially when the only other one we can truly mimic is his enemy.

Just the other day, I watched my daughters push and hit each other because they both wanted to "be the red triangle" in the book they were reading.

"Girls, stop," I said.

No response.

"Girls! Stop!"

Still nothing.

Fire surged through my nostrils as I stomped over and roughly separated the small children.

"GIIIIIIIIIIIIRLS! STOOOOOP!"

If God hadn't been looking, he might have believed that Satan had sneaked into my soul. The mannerisms were that spot on. Even my voice changed to copy the Enemy.

It was terrifying.

And, for God, it was probably downright infuriating.

"Daughter," he whispered, "I love you most when you're most like you."

I finally unclenched my teeth. "What do you mean?"

My Father glanced into my face and his heart ached. It begged for me to cherish and protect who I am, the way he does. He pleaded for me to remember who I am at my core—a human made in God's own image. A girl made to be godly.

"I created you in my image and likeness." He exhaled and shrugged. "When you become like someone else, you and I both disappear."

SNACK TIME!

Spend some time sitting before Jesus in the Blessed Sacrament, and then ask for the grace to imitate him.

PRAYER

God, you are so incredibly beautiful. Everything our hearts long for, you are. You are the source of Goodness itself and all good in this world comes as a reflection of you. Father, your creation is saturated with your infinite wisdom and creativity. Jesus, your Sacred Heart is full of tender mercy, patience, and love. Holy Spirit, your generosity and helpfulness inspire me to action. Holy Trinity, I want to be more like you. Grow in me the goodness that emanates from you. Fill me with the virtues that find their birth in your existence. Let me be a clear reflection of you, now and forever. Amen.

22

"Keep Making That Face and It'll Freeze That Way"

Seeing God's Beauty in Yourself

"You are altogether beautiful, my love;
there is no flaw in you" (Song of Solomon 4:7).

My husband and I went on a date night to a place that teaches you how to paint. In one night, they were to transform us into professional painters. Okay, well, maybe not professional painters, but if my work didn't end up looking like my one-year-old had done it, that would be progress enough for me.

When we got there, we took a seat, and the instructor took us step-by-step through mixing paints together on the canvas to create a perfect peach sunset.

"When you like the way it looks, STOP painting," she said into her microphone.

Unsure, I globbed some bright yellow paint onto my canvas, threw in a touch of red, then glazed over all of it with white. Before I knew it, I actually liked the way it looked. So, I stopped.

"Okay," the teacher said. "Now we're going to use black. Be very careful with black because it's really hard to fix if you mess up."

Gulp.

My hands trembled as I tried to draw a shadowy palm tree.

Don't mess up, don't mess up, don't mess up.

I glanced over at my husband's art and marveled. His leaves were wispy and fun. The color of his ocean was perfectly realistic. His sun actually appeared to be slipping below the horizon. It was beautiful.

Then I looked at mine. My leaves were much bulkier, my sun was way bigger, and my white flecks on the ocean looked more like worms than sparkles on the water.

But I had done it. And it actually looked like a sunset. It was beautiful.

The same is true with us—me and you. And our children too—all of humanity, really.

You see, God was the artist who created us. He used all sorts of brushes and infinite shades of color. He scrutinized each detail of who we are, and he was very intentional with his work. The colors of our hair, the shapes of our noses, the length and width of our bodies. What we like, what we don't like. Our strengths and weaknesses. Everything. He put it all together, step-by-step, according to his own vision of how we should look.

Yet, I often glance over at others and marvel. Their hair is fashionable and fun. The color and smoothness of their skin, perfect. Their eye color, unique and intriguing. Each of them actually looks like a God-made masterpiece. Because they are. They're beautiful.

Then I look at myself. In my mind, my body is much bulkier, some parts of me way too big, other parts of me too small. But God made me, too. And when I remember that, I realize I actually look like a God-made masterpiece. Because I am. It's beautiful.

I imagine that after all his work mixing us together, stroke by stroke, paint by paint, God looked at each and every one of us and marveled.

To him, we were altogether beautiful.

And when he liked the way we looked, he stopped painting.

SNACK TIME!

Take a moment to thank God for creating you the way he did, and ask him to help you see yourself as he does.

PRAYER

You say I am beautiful and that there is no flaw in me, but sometimes I struggle to see that. Give me eyes to see myself the way you see me. Instead of seeing faults in my body, let me see your thumbprint. Remind me that I did nothing to grow or create these parts of my body that I have difficulty with;

rather, I received them from you—the very source of Beauty itself. Everything you do has meaning. Even the tiniest details are not overlooked by you. To you, and through you, every bit matters, including every inch of my body, which you formed in my mother's womb. Help me remember that every part of me matters. Every inch of me was discerned. And when you deemed me beautiful, I came into existence. Amen.

23

"No Use Crying over Spilled Milk"

The Beauty of Scars and Stretch Marks

"By his bruises we are healed" (Isaiah 53:5).

It's been really difficult to get my body back after having babies.

My legs are covered in bumpy, clumpy varicose veins. The skin around my stomach sags and dimples, and my belly button has transformed from a taut innie to a stretched-out patch of dangly skin. Not to mention, my tummy pudges from too many chicken nuggets and too little time to exercise, and my front teeth have been knocked crooked by too many bucking toddler heads.

Not gonna lie, it's been hard to learn to love.

So, instead, I learned to cover it all up.

But the other day, as I ran around the house playing tag with my three-year-old, the girl trapped me in my bedroom. There I was, crouching beside my bed while she stood in the doorway, blocking my escape.

With a wild giggle, she charged at me. I screeched my surrender, then picked her up, and we both flopped backward onto the soft mattress. She curled into me then, relishing the chance to snuggle with Mom. But during our topple, my shirt crept up above my belly button, exposing all my battle scars.

"What's this?" My daughter studied my stomach with a crinkled brow, and then placed her tiny fingers over the wounds.

My cheeks flushed in humiliation, but I resisted the urge to yank my shirt down. Instead, I let her examine the wounds—the very ones I earned by bringing her life into the world.

As she wiggled the skin around my belly, a smile spread across her face. She looked up at me then, her eyes sparkling. "I like this. It's beautiful."

I did a double take at her words. Never did I think someone would call my body beautiful after the way it has morphed over the years from having so many babies.

So that night, when no one was looking, I peeked in the mirror at the saggy skin around my middle. I wiggled it the same way she had, and squinted at my reflection, trying to see what she saw. But it was useless. *What on earth could she have found beautiful about this?* I wondered.

Then, on a whim, I picked up my rosary.

I began praying each decade, one after the other, following along in a beat-up book of Rosary reflections until I came upon a prayer about how Jesus now sits at the right hand of the Father, his wounds an eternal plea on our behalf.

I sat in shock, contemplating that image.

In that moment, I realized that Jesus' entire body was covered in scars. Dots of blood spotted his forehead where the crown of thorns pierced his scalp. Long, ragged stripes ran across his whole body from the scourging. His shoulders screamed with bruises and scratches from his heavy, splintered cross. Not to mention, the holes in his hands, feet, and side forever sing of the thick spikes that bound him to the cross and the spear that finished the job.

His back, his arms, his legs—his whole body—must've been streaked and striped.

And what did he do with those scars? He now sits at the right hand of the Father, unashamedly exposing every single one of them in a desperate plea. For me. For you. For all of us.

His scars redeem. His scars heal. His scars are our way to heaven. And, because of that, they are scars he'd never dream of hiding. Not in a million years.

I ran to grab a crucifix, and, with a heart engulfed in admiration, I examined the wounds he earned by bringing my life into the world. As I traced my thumb along his scars, a smile spread across my face. I looked at him, my eyes sparkling with tears. "Jesus, I love you. You're beautiful."

SNACK TIME!

Every time you see the marks left behind by motherhood, let them remind you of Jesus and how his scars redeem you.

PRAYER

God, help me resist the urge to hide myself from you. Instead of concealing the marks that cover my body, I willingly expose them and bring them to you, Father, praying that they may be an appeal to you. Please, Lord, I beg you to remember the most selfless act I've done with my life—the ongoing sacrifice of laying down my life for my children. This act unites me with you, Jesus. Because of the glorious works you accomplished through your Passion, my scars are not hideous, but redemptive. So, instead of hiding my scars, help me grow closer to you through them. Amen.

24

"The Best of Both Worlds"

God Created Us Body and Soul

"See, I have inscribed you on the palms of my hands"
(Isaiah 49:16).

Not long ago, we went to a birthday party at Cici's Pizza.

Immediately, the flashing arcade lights beckoned to the children, and off they ran together, carrying baggies of coins, eager to win little prizes.

"Do you have any money, Mommy?" my daughters asked, almost in unison.

I cringed at the hope in their voices.

"I don't know . . ." I stammered. "Let me check."

The girls danced in front of me, clapping with joy. The pressure was officially on.

I unzipped my bag, said a quick prayer, and eventually scrounged up a little change for them both.

With smiles and thanks, they dashed off to join their friends. Moments later, they returned, their smiles somehow even bigger than before.

"Mom! Guess what we got!" they said, the big surprise concealed in each tiny, closed fist. Their coins were gone. They'd spent everything on whatever was hiding in their hands.

"What?"

"Diamonds!" They uncurled their fingers, displaying the shiny new gems, enclosed safely in a plastic container.

I feigned a gasp. "Wow! How beautiful!"

"Can I take mine out and hold it?" my youngest asked.

"Of course, but be careful. We don't want to lose it."

My three-year-old nodded solemnly, sealing her oath with a death grip on her finest jewel.

For days, the kids went everywhere—and I mean *everywhere*—with those cherished diamonds tucked tightly into the crevices of their palms.

It got me thinking about us—about you and me and all of humanity.

About how when God made people, he put a small piece of himself inside every single one of us. This immortal sliver of divinity—our soul—glitters and shines from within us, like an invaluable jewel.

I turned to my five-year-old, whose immortal, glittering diamond is older than most.

"What do you like about your diamond?" I asked.

"It's just so beautiful," she said with a sigh. "I love it."

"And what about the case? Why not just throw that away?" I prodded. "What makes the case so special?"

She lifted her prized possession and peered at the glorious jewel with awe. "I like it because it keeps my diamond safe."

A smile spread onto my face as I nodded in agreement. "I couldn't have said it better myself, kiddo."

You see, God's not dumb. He knows that a treasure like our soul needs protecting. There's an enemy working hard to distract us from that part of ourselves, to convince us to defile it, or to let him flat out rob it from us.

So God gave us *two* treasures: a glittering diamond *and* a protective covering. A divine gem (our soul) and its equally important counterpart (our body) that allows us to express our soul.

God knows precisely how precious these gifts are. So much so, that our Father gave his Son everything that he needed to win the prize of humanity: he gave him a human body in the Incarnation. And because of Jesus' incredible love for us, he took what he was given and spent it all. Every breath, every droplet of blood. He spent it. For you. For me. For every single one of us.

And, after giving up everything he had, he returned to the Father with a smile somehow bigger than ever before.

I can just imagine their exchange.

"Look what I got," Jesus must have said, the big surprise concealed within the wounds on his wrists.

"What?"

"*All* the diamonds."

"How beautiful!" the Father would exclaim with genuine admiration. "But be careful. We don't want to lose any of them."

And then Jesus would nod, sealing his oath with a firm grip on his finest jewels, so he could go everywhere—and I mean *everywhere*—with those cherished diamonds tucked tightly into the crevices of his palms.

SNACK TIME!

Have you ever considered that taking care of your body can help you take care of your soul? What is one way you can do this today?

PRAYER

Lord, help me remember that I have an immortal jewel—a sliver of divinity—inside me. One that was handcrafted and given to me by you. My soul is so valuable that you literally died to protect it. Thank you, Jesus, for such an incredible gift and for spending everything you had on me. Bring me to my knees now in awe of your limitless love and give me the ability to humbly receive such a priceless gift. You—the Almighty Immortal One—became flesh, died, were buried, and came back to life. Let me ponder those miraculous ways in which you worked to protect my soul and raise my body on the last day. You spent everything for me. Now, God, I pray that you'll help me do what I can to continue your mission. Give me the strength to spend everything I have for you. Amen.

PART IV

You Can Have It All Without Waiting "Until They're Older"

25

"Go Ask Your Father"

Praying While You're in the Trenches

"Pray in the Spirit at all times in every prayer and supplication" (Ephesians 6:18).

My kids have this uncanny, semi-supernatural ability to know the moment I wake up. It doesn't matter how old they are. To them, the sound of my eyes opening is their alarm clock.

When I had my first baby, I naively tried to wake up before everyone else to soak up the silence of the house with a cup of coffee and my Bible. Darkness pressed in from the windows. Everything was still. No one could possibly be awake at this God-forsaken time of day.

I smiled.

As quietly as I could, I brewed some coffee and then joyfully flopped down in a cozy chair as far away from the nursery as possible. After covering my lap with a soft blanket and inhaling the sweet warmth rising from my mug, I cracked open Scripture.

"Waaaaah!!" the baby cried from her crib.

And just like that, my quiet prayer time was over for the day.

Surely that was a fluke, I grumbled to myself as I nursed the baby. *I'll try again tomorrow.*

Well, tomorrow came, and the day after that. And the day after that, and the day after that. Each and every time, the baby foiled my plans for a quiet morning with God.

I huffed my frustration.

In my mind, quality prayer time with God meant lengthy time together. Quiet, calm time. Time to breathe and think and *be*.

But I didn't have that kind of time anymore, even when I tried to carve it into the schedule.

This is impossible, I thought, exhausted from the longer-than-normal days. *I'm going to sleep in, and if the baby needs something, my husband can get her.*

The next day, I woke an hour later than normal, and rolled over to find my husband—and the baby—still sleeping.

Maybe the baby had worn herself out with all those early mornings, too. Maybe she'd sleep in a bit longer. Fueled with hope, I sprang silently out of bed, brewed a single cup of coffee, and rushed to my chair. I inhaled the sweet warmth rising from my mug and cracked open Scripture.

"Waaaaaaaah!!" the baby cried from her crib.

"Are you kidding me, God?" I whined, slamming my Bible down beside me. "How can we keep our relationship strong if we never have time together?"

To answer that question, God gave me another baby.

And then another. Aaaand another.

Eventually, out of exhaustion and defeat, I stopped trying to wake up early. Stopped trying to have quiet, quality time with my Beloved. It only made the days longer. Harder. Less spiritually fulfilled.

Little did I know that my fourth baby would teach me how to pray.

Now she's two years old and her prayer life is stronger than anyone else's. She's *always* talking to God, telling Jesus whatever is on her little heart. Sometimes her prayer is lengthy. Sometimes it's gibberish. But mostly, it's 3.4 seconds of talking to God because that's as long as her little two-year-old brain can focus on something.

"Jesus, can I talk to you?" she asks aloud.

I clear my throat and drop an octave to my Jesus-y man-voice. "Of course," I say. "You can always talk to me."

Then she does it. She prays. Freely. Wholeheartedly. Way better than me.

She doesn't need peace and quiet. Heck, as the fourth child in our family, she doesn't even know what peace and quiet is. All she's got is 3.4 seconds, and that's all she needs.

In those 3.4 seconds, she acknowledges God's presence in her life, telling Jesus all about what happened in her day. Eating breakfast. Sliding down a slide. Riding the animals—ahem, the *carousel*—at the zoo. "'Member dat, Jesus?" she asks, fully aware that Jesus was right there with her through it all.

In 3.4 seconds, she invites God to be with her. "Will you read book to me, Jesus?"

In 3.4 seconds, she asks God's thoughts about things. "You like my shirt, Jesus?"

In 3.4 seconds, she asks for his help. "Help my boo boo better, Jesus!"

In 3.4 seconds, she tells him how much she loves him. "Jesus, I love you so, so, sooooo much."

In 3.4 seconds, she even consoles his Sacred Heart. "Jesus, your boo boos ouchie?" she says, cradling the crucifix, her brows scrunched in compassion. "I kiss them better." And sure enough, she puts her lips to his wounds.

It may only be 3.4 seconds at a time—and a hectic, loud 3.4 seconds at that—but she always, always treats Jesus as her friend.

And that, I realized, was prayer. That was the treasure. It doesn't have to be lengthy. It doesn't have to be fancy. Heck, it doesn't even have to be quiet. It just has to *be*.

Now, thanks to my toddler, my prayer life is stronger than ever. I'm always talking to God. Sometimes it's lengthy. Sometimes it's gibberish. But mostly, it's 3.4 seconds of talking to God because that's as long as my tired, interrupted brain can focus on something.

In those 3.4 seconds, I acknowledge God's presence in my life. "Thanks for such a beautiful day, Jesus."

In 3.4 seconds, I invite God to be with me. "Come, Holy Spirit."

In 3.4 seconds, I ask God's thoughts about things. "Is this show okay for me to watch, Jesus?"

In 3.4 seconds, I ask for his help. "Jesus, help me be patient."

In 3.4 seconds, I tell him how much I love him. "Wow, God, you are so awesome."

In 3.4 seconds, I console him. "How can I help you today, Jesus?"

It may only be 3.4 seconds at a time—and a hectic, loud 3.4 seconds at that—but it's finally, finally treating Jesus as a friend.

SNACK TIME!

Talk to Jesus as a friend, even if you only have 3.4 seconds at a time.

PRAYER

Jesus, I love when we get to have quality time—when life is quiet and you and I get to be together, uninterrupted—but this season of life rarely allows me to sit with you for great lengths of time. There's little time to listen. There's little calm and even less quiet. When I do have a quick moment, I find myself feeling rushed, anticipating the next cry, the next interruption, the next problem that requires my assistance. Instead of lamenting this loss, help me rejoice in the truth that you are always with me. Remind me to turn your way, however briefly. Help me stay close to you throughout this season so that when my children are grown, I can continue to come to you, my heart fully connected to yours as we reminisce about these days. When that time comes, grant me the confidence and familiarity to ask, "'Member dat, Jesus?"

26

"The World Doesn't Revolve Around You"

The Importance of Serving

"So if I, your Lord and Teacher, have washed your feet,
you also ought to wash one another's feet" (John 13:14).

Lately, my kids have been a choir of desire, constantly listing all their wants and demands before me. It's true they need my permission and my help to get the things they want, but the majority of their words expose their single-minded focus on themselves. All day long, all I hear is:

"Can I have . . . ?"

"Give me . . ."

"I really want (insert everything in the entire world here)."

They look to me, expecting me to fulfill all their wishes as though I were a magic genie instead of their mother.

To be honest, I have no idea where they got that idea. My inclination toward selfish behavior is to take things *away*, not lavish my kids with *more* stuff. And definitely not stuff they *want*.

But still, they look to me, knowing that I love them and want to give them good things.

The other day, for example, my kids swarmed me as I was making some final touches on dinner.

"Can I have the green plate?" one daughter shouted.

My other daughter ransacked the utensil drawer. "I want the Doc fork!"

"*I* like Doc fork!" my two-year-old wailed.

I spun on my heels (which is hard to do when you're both hugely pregnant and surrounded on all sides by tiny people). Then I shut the drawer, letting the dinner hiss and crackle in the pan behind me.

"Whoa, whoa, whoa," I shouted above the noise. "Do you think having a specific plate or fork will make you any happier in life?"

They shook their heads, but still clung tightly to their treasures.

"Instead of asking for what more you can *have*, why don't you ask how you can *help*?"

In shock, I watched them obey.

My oldest poured milk for everyone and distributed the cups. My middle set the table, putting plates in their places and divvying up the utensils, going so far as to willingly give the beloved Doc McStuffins fork to her little brother.

And the result?

Joy. Trust. Unity. Love.

Heaven. It was a glimpse of heaven.

Selfishness—the attempt to get everything we want—is really the assassin of those things. Under a false promise of joy, focusing on getting what we want only produces dissatisfaction.

But, man, isn't that how *I* operate?

I'm a one-woman choir of desire, constantly thinking about what I want and listing my demands before the Father. It's true I need his help to get the things I want, but the majority of my words expose my single-minded focus on myself. All day long, all he hears is:

"Can I have . . . ?"

"Give me . . ."

"I really want (insert everything in the entire world here)."

Every day, I put all my plans, all my desires, all my wants before God. Which is fine and good. He wants us to tell him what's on our hearts. But how often do my conversations with God stop there? How often do I overlook everything he's given me so far?

I look to him, asking for more and expecting him to fulfill all my wishes as though he were a magic genie instead of my Father. To be honest, I have no idea where

I got that idea. His inclination toward my prideful, self-ish behavior is to humble me. And when I ask for patience or humility, he doesn't just zap those virtues into my heart. He gives me trying experiences that require me to practice them.

But still, I look to him, knowing that he loves me and wants to give me good things.

"Whoa, whoa, whoa," God whispers. "Instead of asking what you can *have*, why don't you ask how you can *help*?"

Then I see the truth of my situation.

My time. My talents. My treasures. My whole *life*.

What have I done to create or provide any of them? I am merely the recipient of those things.

They were all gifts, given to me by my Father who likes to give me good things.

And even though I want to cling to them, I'm learning how to let go and give them to others.

When all I want is a moment to myself, but my kids invite me to play with them, I have the opportunity to give them the gift of my time.

When I'm exhausted after a long day, but the kids need to be fed and bathed, I have the opportunity to give them the gift of my remaining energy.

When I have more food on my plate, but my kids or husband are still hungry, I have the opportunity to give them the gift of a few extra bites.

When everything is *finally* quiet at the end of the night and all I want to do is sit and watch TV, but I choose to pray a Rosary instead, I have the chance to give God the gift of my heart.

When a friend is sick or has a new baby and I want to cook them a meal on my own, but my kids want to help me, we all get the opportunity to practice sharing our time, talents, and treasures together.

The result?

Joy. Trust. Unity. Love.

Heaven. It's a glimpse of heaven.

SNACK TIME!

Joyfully serve your kids and spouse before yourself and encourage your kids to put others first, too.

PRAYER

Lord, help me look around and see everything as a gift from you. My husband. My children. My home and everything in it. Even the very breath in my lungs. Though I take them for granted sometimes, help me remember that I am merely the receiver of your gifts. God, please help me to be a good steward of each and every one of them. My children are your children. My husband, your creation. Everything I have is on loan. Please move in me. Inspire me to give back to you freely. May my life, through you, be a gift to others. My time. My things. My talents. All of it. Help me give it back to you through serving and loving others. Help me to teach my children by word and deed how to serve others joyfully, so that my life—and my family—will become proof that you exist. Amen.

27

"I Had to Walk Uphill in the Snow Both Ways"

Jesus Worked Hard for Us

> "Then he said to them all, 'If any want to become my followers, let them deny themselves and take up their cross daily and follow me'" (Luke 9:23).

"Ready for church?"

It was a silly question, really, and to be honest, I'm not sure why I asked. I gazed upon my two small daughters as they shoved pancakes into their mouths, the stringy syrup striping their pajamas. Cheeks puffed with pastries, they shook their heads.

I ran through the mental checklist: Clean the table. Clean the kids. Dress the kids. Do their hair. Get myself ready. Get out the door.

I quickly glanced at the clock and did the math. Ten minutes. We had to accomplish all of that in ten minutes.

Anxiety stabbed me in the gut. "Time to get dressed! Go, go, go!"

They rose from the table and I heard the *pop* as they pried their syrupy fingers from their plates. As they scurried toward their room, fiddling with everything they could on the way, I saw even from a distance how their hands stuck to whatever they touched. Their toys. The walls. . . .

I cringed.

Wipe down the whole house, I mentally added to the to-do list.

My husband took the baby while I hurried to the bedroom to throw on my Sunday best. After slapping some makeup on my face, I scrambled back to my daughters' room to find them swinging from their bunk beds. Naked.

"Why aren't you dressed?"

They pointed to the closet where their dresses hung. "We couldn't reach."

I glanced down at my watch. Two minutes. With a little luck and a lot of Jesus, we could do this.

The girls chose their dresses and I stuffed them in, zipped them up, then shooed them out the door and into the van. In those few minutes, my husband had also managed—by some miracle of his own—to dress himself, dress the baby, fill a bag with Cheerios, and meet us in the garage.

Quickly, we threw the girls into their car seats and fastened the buckles. Then we were off. As we pulled out of the driveway, my husband and I sighed deeply. Just like we do *every* Sunday.

At church, we piled into our normal seats in the front row. We enjoy the clear view. The few distractions. The public humiliation.

"Mom, I'm hungry," my four-year-old whined.

"What?" I hissed in disbelief. "You just ate breakfast."

"But I'm still hungry. Can I have a snack?"

I grabbed the bulging bag of Cheerios—the one my husband filled before we left home—and handed it over.

Then we were instructed to greet our neighbors. Which we did.

Then came the music. Which we sang.

Then an hour of stillness. Which we can't do to save our souls.

Almost immediately, my daughter dropped the snack bag, scattering eight thousand tiny Os all over the floor. My two-year-old, who was already down there crawling under the pews, picked them up and shoveled them into her mouth. I bent over to clean everything up and my infant son cried out for milk. I sat back up, swung my nursing cover over my head, and exposed myself beneath it so he could eat.

We'd already caused a scene. People were looking. I could feel their gazes smothering the back of my neck. I had no idea what the priest was saying. All I knew was that I was sweating, and if my baby yanked the blanket (as he'd been known to do), the entire congregation would get to see more than just *Jesus'* body today.

My insides squirmed more than my active toddlers. "Do you SEE what I go through to bring my kids to Mass?" I silently whined to God. "Do you see everything I'm doing to be here with you?"

"Really?" The word—definitely not my own—flashed through my mind, along with an image of the crucifix. "I went through some stuff to be here, too . . ."

In one swift, sobering moment, Jesus himself reminded me that my biggest inconveniences are merely that—inconveniences. What I go through—these hardships I can hardly bear—are nothing compared to the absolute agony and misery that Jesus willingly endured. All so he could be here and live up to who he truly is.

Emmanuel. God with us.

SNACK TIME!

The next time you take your kids to Mass, tell them about how hard God worked to be there, too.

PRAYER

Jesus, thank you for working so hard for my sake. You never took the easy way out. Instead, you perfectly obeyed your Father's will, even to the point of death. Before I was born, your eyes were upon me. You endured rejection for my sake. You endured hatred and humiliation for my sake. You endured the agony of the cross for my sake. You gloriously rose from the dead for my sake. And you did it all so you could be here with me now, my God. My Emmanuel. Love, not petty obligation, propelled you every step of the way. Urged on by that same love, let me work to meet you where you are. Help me to pick up my cross and run to you. Amen.

28

"No Pain, No Gain"

We Can Work Hard for Jesus

"He said to them, 'The harvest is plentiful, but the laborers are few; therefore ask the Lord of the harvest to send out laborers into his harvest'" (Luke 10:2).

"Can we go to Mass every day this week?"

The question floated sweetly to my ears on a whisper from my oldest child's lips.

I glanced down at her cute little face—the one radiating innocent joy as she looked up at me, hopeful that I might say yes.

At that time, we were going through a rough spell. The kids rarely listened, let alone obeyed me. They constantly bickered and fought with each other. Not to mention, I was in the first trimester of pregnancy and the only thing I'd done for myself was sit on the couch for a couple minutes when sickness knocked me off my feet.

Just thinking about taking all the kids to Mass by myself made the nausea churn in my stomach.

But how could I say no to a request like that?

The next morning, we were dressed and out the door early, armed with water cups, snacks, and the naive confidence that I. Could. Do. This.

The two oldest followed me down the aisle, and we all genuflected in front of the tabernacle before sliding into our usual seats in the first pew.

So far, so good.

I let out a sigh of relief. Maybe I really could do this.

The ceremony began.

Father processed down the aisle.

Everyone sang a beautiful hymn.

The lector started the first Scripture reading.

And then my two-year-old went crazy. He bucked and kicked, screamed and hit as though we were there for his own personal exorcism.

But I couldn't take him out into the lobby and leave my two young girls sitting in the pew. And I definitely didn't want to do the walk of shame with ALL my children from the front of the sanctuary to the back. So, I wrestled with my toddler, shushing into his ear, praying to God that he would calm down.

But apparently even God couldn't hear me above the demonic noises we were making.

Meanwhile, my youngest daughter realized that she could start picking fights with her older sister. And, in the span of one of my racing heartbeats, we became a crazy, uncontrollable train wreck.

Internally, I cursed Confident Me for thinking this could ever have been possible.

The back of my neck flushed beneath everyone's stares as I imagined their eyes searing my skin with scorn.

Why would she bring those children here if she can't control them?

I can't hear a thing the priest is saying.

They should have stayed home. They're ruining the Mass for everyone else.

I shook these thoughts from my mind and sat in my seat, dodging my son's bucking head and flying fists, blotting the sweat from my forehead and focusing all my energy on holding back the tears that threatened to pour down my cheeks. After all, the only thing that could be more humiliating would be to start *crying*, for goodness' sake.

And then our sweet, sweet priest stopped mid-homily and looked directly at me.

"Thank you for bringing your children to Mass today," he said in his gentle, loving way. Into his microphone. For all to hear.

Couldn't he see that I was trying *NOT* to cry?

The rest of the Mass went by in a blur. Literally. Tears piled high, testing the strength of my eyelids and my stubborn will.

Afterward, several ladies approached us, thanking me for bringing my kids to Mass, assuring me that it's okay if they make noise. I thanked them with a quick nod and then rushed out the door.

When we got to the car, my four-year-old whined about not getting to go to the park—their treat for doing well at Mass.

That was it. Battle lost. Tears came flooding down uncontrollably as I wallowed in my failure. Failure to control my kids. Failure to go to Mass with my kids. Failure to be a good mom.

The hunger for Jesus still lingered. I knew I needed him now—in my weakness—more than ever. But never again could I go through what I had just endured.

I simply wasn't strong enough.

So I wept all the way home as my children stared at me, silent—for once—and absolutely horrified. Never before had they seen their mom cry, and boy, was she unleashing it now.

When we got home, I told the kids I needed some time to myself, and then I shut myself in my closet and cried more.

All alone, I lamented to Jesus about how badly I wanted him, but how I just couldn't do it. Not with children.

Then, to my astonishment, Jesus replied.

"How much do you really want me?" he asked. "Enough to be humiliated?"

I paused in both shock and thought.

"You were worth the humiliation to me," he added.

At that point, I realized my answer had been no.

No, I did not want him enough to be humiliated.

No, I did not want him enough to have to *work* to receive him in the Eucharist.

No, I did not want him enough to endure scornful looks.

No, he was not worth the sweat, the tears, the embarrassment.

But after being called out, I realized that my answer—like Mary's—had to become yes.

The next day, I took my children to Mass again. Then again the day after that, and the day after that. Now, on average, we try to make it three times each week.

Some days my kids participate, singing, kneeling, and responding as they ought. Some days my son sings the Alleluia louder than the entire congregation put together. Some days, my youngest daughter asks if she can offer a prayer request during the Prayers of the Faithful. My heart explodes on those days, as I thank God for the works he is doing in my children through the gift of the Mass.

On other days, my kids bicker and fight. Those days my son runs down the pew and I have to chase him and wrestle him back to our seat. Those days I get poked in the face. A lot. One day, my son even discovered that his finger fits perfectly inside my ear.

Yet somehow, I now look forward to those harder days.

Then, as I kneel before the Eucharist, I can offer Jesus my humiliation, my embarrassment, and my weak, tired body. It is then that I can truly show Jesus how much I want him.

And only then—when I am at my weakest—can I truly taste the rich, saving sweetness of the Bread of Life.

SNACK TIME!

How much do you want Jesus? Enough to face humiliation? Enough to work to receive him in the Eucharist?

You were worth the pain and exhaustion to him.

PRAYER

Lord, how can it be that I was worth the cross? That I was worth the humiliation? The torture? The pain? How can it be that you chose to endure it all when I—someone who is here today and gone tomorrow—was the prize? You, Lord, are the ultimate prize. The greatest gift. I choose you. When my children act out, help me pursue you still. When I am tired, help me pursue you still. When I am rejected, help me pursue you still. When I am crushed beneath the weight of my cross, help me pursue you still. Like your sweet Mother, may my answer to you always be yes. Lord, I choose you alone as my inheritance. You are my prize, my pleasure, and my portion. You, to me, are worth everything. Amen.

29

"You Can Lead a Horse to Water, but You Can't Make Him Drink"

Choosing to Go to Confession

"Wash me thoroughly from my iniquity,
and cleanse me from my sin" (Psalm 51:2).

For some reason, my kids hate getting clean.

They love *playing* in water, don't get me wrong, but by golly, the moment they see soap, all hell breaks loose.

I've never understood it, really. I, personally, love the squeaky fresh feeling right after I step out of the shower. Hair sopping wet, rinsed free of its typical filth, my skin sticky with dampness and purity. It's like taking a deep breath of fresh air after hanging out in a dank tomb for a bit.

Maybe that's because, in this season of life, I tend to spend more time caked in layers of dirt than I do washing it all off.

Whatever the case, my kids don't seem to cherish that feeling as much as I do. They're too busy playing

with toys. Too busy splashing water all over the bathroom. Too busy swimming as far from me as possible to
the other side of the bathtub.

But after a particularly long, tiring, get-yourself-
dirty kind of day, I stopped trying to grab them. Stopped
trying to wrestle with them. Stopped trying to *make*
them clean.

"Don't you guys want to get clean?" I said with exasperation, throwing my hands in the air and then letting
them crash back down in the murky water. "All you have
to do is sit there, and I'll do all the work."

The two small children looked up at me, wide-eyed,
knowing full well by the level of her desperation that
this would be a good time to listen to Mom.

So they did as they were told and actually sat still—
well, as still as two small children can—while I rubbed
and scrubbed and polished them clean.

As always, I washed them—every inch and crevice—
until not a trace of their stink remained. They were
completely spotless, as though that repugnant sweat and
dirt had never stained their smooth skin. By the time
they emerged from the tub, they practically sparkled.

"See?" I asked, cradling my beaming two-year-old.
"Doesn't it feel good to be clean?"

I watched her nod, but in that moment, it hit me.

For some reason, I myself must actually hate getting
clean. Spiritually, that is.

I love going to church, don't get me wrong, but by golly, the moment I hear "Confession" and "Examination of Conscience," my stomach knots over the hellishness I've let loose.

I've never understood it, really. I love the squeaky fresh feeling right after I step out of the confessional, my soul rinsed free of its typical filth, radiating the light of purity. It's like taking a deep breath of fresh air after hanging out in a dank tomb for a bit.

But in this season of life, I tend to spend more time caked in spiritual layers of dirt than I do actually washing it all off.

I'm too busy scrolling mindlessly on my phone or jotting down ideas for books and blogs. Too busy hectically running my kids here and there—every direction but toward God in the confessional.

But after a particularly long, tiring, get-yourself-dirty kind of season, God stopped trying to grab me. Stopped trying to wrestle with me. Stopped trying to *make* me clean.

"Don't you want to get clean?" he said with exasperation, dropping his wounded hands to his sides. "All you have to do is sit there, and I'll do all the work."

I looked up at him, wide-eyed, knowing full well this would be a good time to listen. It had been such a long time since my last confession, I was morally bound to confess *that*.

So I did as I was told and actually sat still—well, as still as I could as my heart wriggled and squirmed inside me, as it does with all my dirty confessions.

And, as always, God washed me clean—every inch, every crevice—until not one trace of my stink remained. I was completely spotless, as though that repugnant sin had never stained my soul.

By the time I emerged from the confessional, I was practically sparkling.

"See?" God asked, cradling me as I beamed. "Doesn't it feel good to be clean?"

SNACK TIME!

Schedule a time to go to Confession.

PRAYER

Lord Jesus, you who are all pure and good, look upon me with your endless Divine Mercy. In sinning against you, I hold the hammer that drove the nails into your hands and feet. I love you above all things and I detest my sinfulness because it hurts you so. Please, Lord, forgive me and rain down on me the grace to choose you, to love you, and to live my life in a way that honors you. Amen.

30

"It Costs an Arm and a Leg"

Experiencing God Through Our Bodily Senses

"For it was you who formed my inward parts;
   you knit me together in my mother's womb.
I praise you, for I am fearfully and wonderfully made"
(Psalm 139:13–14).

My two-year-old has become obsessed with the bathroom.

She's discovered an innate talent for turning on the faucet and letting it run for hours, and she's also a master at ripping off her diaper whenever she feels like it. But her favorite thing to do is follow her brother into the bathroom while he does his business. Whether he likes having a friend or an audience, I don't know, but he lets her stay with him until he's finished.

Eventually, he calls from the toilet, waiting for me to clean him up.

On cue, I stroll into the small bathroom, now crowded with the three of us, and unroll a few squares of toilet paper. My son leans forward to let me get the job done.

My two-year-old cranes her neck to get a better view. "I see?"

Since we're on the verge of potty training, I hold up the scrunched, soiled paper for her to feast her curious little eyes.

She gasps, truly amazed. Her brother doesn't need a diaper? Everything goes into the toilet? Cleanly? And then you just flush it away?

Wooooow.

I turn to throw the dirty stuff into the toilet, but my two-year-old puts her hand on my shoulder to stop me. She cocks her little head and squints curiously at me. "I smell?"

Disgusted as I am, I laugh out loud. "No, baby, you don't want to smell this. It's yucky."

As I flush the waste away, I can't help but contemplate the beautiful way God created humanity. He intentionally gave us a soul thirsting for its Beloved, and he also gave us a body with senses to explore and investigate everything around us—groping through the world until we've found him.

It's so different from how I used to view my body.

Before I knew Christ, my body was merely a billboard. Something to look at. Something to constantly tweak and perfect in a desperate attempt to attract and impress others. Because of that, in my own mind, my body became a tool—a gauge of perfection. And boy, I was all about being perfect.

But our bodies are not tools. They're not status symbols or something to objectify. They are a part of who we are as humans. They're God's way of giving us the chance to seek, probe, scrutinize, and experience everything around us in our lifelong search for *him*.

Because the truth is, we're just as curious as toddlers. Whether we recognize it or not, everyone is constantly searching for the one thing that will fill the God-shaped hole in our hearts. We're constantly searching for the one thing that will bring us true joy. If we're not careful, though, we can watch or taste or sniff some pretty dirty stuff while trying to find it.

Fortunately for us, God knows we're physical *and* spiritual beings. He created us, for goodness' sake. So, being the good Father that he is, he also gave us physical and spiritual ways of finding him and engaging with him.

Through the gift of the Eucharist, we can cradle him in our palm and taste him on our tongue.

Through the Sacrament of Reconciliation, we can hear his absolution through the mouth of our confessor, and at Mass, we can hear his word proclaimed.

In Baptism, we can feel his cleansing purity washing us free of sin.

We can catch a whiff of the incense as our prayers rise toward heaven.

We can gaze upon Jesus on the cross or in the tabernacle, where his actual body rests securely.

I take a glance in the mirror before turning off the bathroom light and walking away.

"MOOOOOOOOOOOOOOOOOOOOOM!" my two-year-old yells, her hands flailing above her head as she sprints toward me with a huge smile on her face.

I bend down and hold my arms out wide as she crashes into my embrace. Laughter bubbles as we topple backward together. I kiss her cheeks, tickle her sides, and brush her blond, lavender-scented hair from her face.

As we crash to the floor, my rosary slips out of my back pocket.

"Mommy's rosie?" she asks, and I chuckle in admiration of her innocence. "I hold, please?"

I hate the thought of my children wandering toward waste, so I steer my daughter down the path that leads to God. I pick up the rosary and offer it to her, letting her touch the wooden beads and feel the smooth spheres with her fingertips.

In that moment, I find immense, genuine gratitude for our bodies.

What besides my body can I use to kiss, tickle, hug, and hold my children? What better way can I show people I love them? What better way can I experience God and share him with others?

There isn't a plethora of tools I can whip out.

I only have one means to really sense my way through the world toward God and bring my babies along with me: my body.

And I intend to use it well.

SNACK TIME!

Experience God with all five senses.

PRAYER

God, you created humanity. You know that we are physical as well as spiritual beings. Thank you, Lord, for making yourself present and accessible physically and spiritually. Thank you, Creator of the cosmos, for making yourself tangible to someone as small as me. I pray that I may explore you and give you fully to others through the senses you gave me. Through my fingers, let my children feel your touch. Through my words, let them hear your voice. In all I say and do, Lord, be present and palpable. May I always lead my children down the path that leads to you. Amen.

Epilogue

You're Gonna Miss This

For whatever reason, my husband and I decided it'd be a good idea to bring our toddlers to a professional basketball game. He works in the sports industry and I grew up with basketball in my blood. So what the heck? It'd be fun.

Once we got our tickets, we found our seats and squished ourselves into them.

Not too long into the game, the crowd around us roared to life. My husband turned toward me with disbelief in his eyes.

"Did you see that?" he asked.

I quieted the toddler in my lap and shook my head. "No, what?"

He pointed to the jumbotron as the last remnants of replay flashed on the screen. But my lap-child was wiggling again and I looked away to tend to her.

The rest of the basketball game went by in a blur. A blur of giggles, tickles, and removing my children from the cascading cement steps. A fuzzy haze of voices. My voice. Repeating common phrases like "No thank you!" and "Get down from there!"

For all I knew, only four people were in the entire arena. The same four that could have been at home doing the exact same thing.

Except for one man. The beer vendor.

"Looks like you've got your work cut out for you tonight," he chuckled.

I nodded. "*Every* night."

He smiled, a nostalgic look in his middle-aged eyes. "Yeah, well, one day you're gonna miss this."

For a moment, I paused—if for no other reason than to question the man's sanity. Or his rose-tinted glasses. Or whether maybe he'd been drinking a little too much of the stuff in his tub.

After all, what was there to miss? I'd come to watch basketball, a game as much a part of my personal history as the skin I wear on my bones. But even though most of the athletes were as tall as my seven-foot Christmas tree, I had barely even noticed they were there.

Instead, I'd been constantly removing two tiny people from the handrails in the stands.

Miss it? I chortled to myself. *How could I miss it?*

But he's not the only one who's said those words. The message seems to be on the tongue of every parent who has made it out of the trenches. Like they know something we don't. Like they're in some Secret Parent Club and all they're allowed to say is, "You're gonna miss this."

But, honestly, what is there to miss about being covered in someone else's poop, pee, and snot? What's so great about the middle-of-the-night interruptions and early morning wake-up calls? The long days and even longer bedtime routines? How could I mourn the loss of temper tantrums and conniption fits? Or the juggling act with several tiny humans as they all scream that they "need" different things?

How would anyone in their right mind *miss* that stuff?

I spent the second half of the basketball game trying to figure it out.

They've been in my shoes. These new-parent shoes. They know about the long hours, the aching muscles. They understand sleep schedules, picky eaters, constant noise, and the desperate need to throw in the towel some days.

We're looking at parenting—the same exact stage of parenting, in fact—but seeing totally different things.

It's like the story where blind men try to learn about an elephant by touching different parts of the elephant's body. Each man describes the elephant as something different based on which part they touch.

When it comes to parenting, I'm a lot like those blind men, clinging to one part and trying to understand the whole.

What these other parents see, then, isn't rose-tinted. It's more fleshed out—more truthful—because they can see a lot more of the elephant.

At this point in parenting, all I can see is how much my back aches from holding small kids all day. *They know that back pain is nothing compared to the heartbreak when kids get too big to hold.*

I can see how hard I work to entertain my kids all day every day. *They know it takes a lot more than silly faces and tickles to make their children laugh now.*

I see the constant messes of spilled milk, chewed food, and death-trap Legos that I have to clean up. *Their messes involve broken hearts, puberty, and body image issues.*

I see how I have zero personal space or time to myself. *They would give anything to see that little kid come into the room again, even if they were in the middle of doing toilet business. But that little kid doesn't exist anymore.*

I sometimes think I could be so much more—*do* so much more with my life—"if" . . . *They've seen the fruit of parenting and know they've never done anything more important.*

I see tantrums, fights, and uncontrollable whining. *They remember the squeals of joy, the huge level of little-kid excitement, and the infinite hugs and kisses, and they know that to this day, they've never again come so close to pure innocence.*

I see myself getting pulled in so many directions I fear my body might snap. *They know I will never be this pursued, adored, or admired again.*

So, momma, maybe you're wading through a dung pile trying to figure out this whole elephant thing. But keep in mind that you might not be seeing the whole picture.

The bigger picture is that you have a front row seat to your little person's life story. There's only one ticket, and it's got your name on it.

Toward the end of the basketball game, my husband's question changed. He knew I hadn't seen the pass down the lane. The last-second shot. The momentum shift toward our favorite team's victory.

This time, his face was full of sympathy. Sorrow, even.

"Are you getting to see any of this?" he asked.

I gazed back at the little person wiggling in my lap. The one whose smile could light up the entire arena, but who instead was begging for me to notice her. Out of everything around her—the lights, the noise, the food, the excitement—all she wanted was me.

"No," I said with a shrug. "But that's okay."

So will I miss it when they're grown? I don't know. Probably.

All I know for certain is that if I don't pay attention, I'll miss it now.

Personal Reflection/ Group Discussion Questions

These guidelines are provided to help inspire your personal prayer or to be used for group discussion. Each set of questions has been specifically selected as a good stopping point for reflection and/or discussion, so you may find it helpful to read the chapter it is based on ahead of time. However, each guide can also be prayed with independently in any order you choose. If you are using the guide in a group setting, you could take some time to reflect on the questions on your own and jot down a few notes before you discuss them as a group. Feel free to use the prayer at the end of each chapter as a closing prayer for your reflection time or group meeting.

PART I: WHAT IS PARENTHOOD?

Nurturing Virtue and Uprooting Vice
Prayer and Discussion Guide for Chapter Two

Motherhood is nothing like a corporate job. There's no one-size-fits-all approach to motherhood. No specific rules or templates. No goals or benchmarks to hit.

Instead, motherhood relies on what you think will be best for your family. Should you bottle feed or breast-feed? Should you stay home or be a working mom? What kinds of food should you allow your kids to eat? How much screen time should they get? What kind of school should they go to? Do they really need to wear shoes? FOR THE LOVE OF ALL THINGS GOOD, WHERE ARE THEIR SHOES?

Whew, the constant decision-making we must do as mothers can be exhausting, especially when it feels as though the fate of our children depends on our getting everything right.

But being a mother is more like being a novice gardener. During the early years, we find ourselves clueless, covered in filth, wondering if our seedlings will grow into the strong, flourishing plants we hope they'll become. Yet, as we make our decisions and do our work, all we can see is the dirt. We don't know which seeds will sprout and produce fruit. All we can do is try our hardest to make the soil as nutrient rich as possible and let God do the rest.

Take some time to prayerfully read Matthew 13:3–23. Pay attention to how you interiorly react to the passage. What is stirring in your heart as you engage with Jesus' words?

Ponder the following questions in the light of the Holy Spirit:

1. What is the soil of your heart like today? Dry and rocky? Moist and rich? What do you want it to look like?

2. What vices (i.e., selfishness, greed, quickness to anger, distractedness, laziness, jealousy, impatience, etc.) do you need God's help to root out?

3. What virtues (i.e., charity, humility, patience, compassion, wisdom, self-control, peacefulness, service, forgiveness, gratitude, prayerfulness, etc.) are already growing in your soul? Which would you like to cultivate more?

4. What kinds of tools (i.e., Scripture, prayer, the sacraments, spiritual reading, etc.) has God used to nurture you in your personal faith life? How has he nurtured your family? What tools do you want to take up in tending to the garden of your family?

The Corporal Works of Mercy
Prayer and Discussion Guide for Chapter Five

The fact that we even *have* the Corporal Works of Mercy is a mercy from God. He gave them to us to show how to love others and imitate Christ more closely. In a way, they're instructions on how to treat everyone the way he would treat them. As you perform the typical tasks of motherhood, witness how your everyday deeds echo those holy acts of service. By accomplishing the daily duties of motherhood, you are living out Scripture and giving the gift of mercy to your family. In this way, even small, mundane tasks like making a peanut butter sandwich, folding laundry, or bringing your kids home from school can become a giant gift of love.

Take some time to pray with the Corporal Works of Mercy outlined in Isaiah 58:1–9 and Matthew 25:35–46. Notice what is important to God in these passages and what the text stirs in your heart.

1. In the light of these Scriptures, think back over some of your experiences as parent. How has your vocation as a mother helped you:

    1) Feed the hungry?
    2) Give drink to the thirsty?
    3) Clothe the naked?
    4) Shelter the homeless?
    5) Visit the sick?
    6) Visit the imprisoned?
    7) Bury the dead?

2. How is God inviting you to manifest mercy in your life today?

What to Do When You Feel Invisible
Prayer and Discussion Guide for Chapter Seven

Have you ever felt completely unseen and unappreciated? Like you're spinning your wheels, sprinting through life at 100 mph and no one even notices? If you're anything like me, the answer is yes. That can make it feel like all your efforts—and, boy, are there a lot of them—mean very little. But take heart in knowing that even when you feel invisible, there is One who loves you so fiercely that he never wants to take his eyes off you.

Prayerfully read about Nathanael's encounter with Jesus (John 1:43–51). Ever wonder what Nathanael was doing under the fig tree that was noteworthy enough for Jesus not only to mention it, but also to call him "a true Israelite with no duplicity"? I like to think that Nathanael may have been praying there, telling God how he felt unseen and unvaluable. So, when Jesus *saw* Nathanael doing that, he proved that God always sees us, even when we feel invisible.

1. What are some areas in your life where you feel overlooked and unappreciated? Is there any-thing you have done recently that has seemingly gone unnoticed?

2. What does Jesus think of these seemingly invis-ible areas of your life?

3. Imagine yourself in Nathanael's place in the Gospel story. How does it feel to hear Jesus speak these words to you today?

I bet God can relate to this feeling of being over-looked and invisible. So many times—at least with me—he has generously given gifts and graces, and I have failed to thank him or even recognize what he has done. But it's never too late to thank God for his blessings.

4. Think of some of the graces God has given you and the things he has done for you. How have you shown him your gratitude? What do you want to thank him for right now?

5. What is one seemingly overlooked task that you can do for God's glory and pleasure? What is one way you can remind yourself to notice God more in your life?

PART II: WHO IS GOD?

Doing What Makes God Happy
Prayer and Discussion Guide for Chapter Eleven

My kids seem to know me really well, which makes sense since they're by my side almost every single moment their eyes are open. They see what I love and what gets under my skin. They know how to make me laugh and they also know how to make me angry. And I, as their parent, know those things about them, too.

Through Jesus' divine teaching, we know that God is our Father. And as in any good parent-child relationship, it's important to get to know him really well. One of the best ways to do this is by diving into Scripture, God's letter to humanity.

Take some time to ask God the Father to reveal himself to you. Then prayerfully read Luke 15:11–32 and Hosea 11:1–4, 8–9.

1. What image comes to mind when you think of God the Father? What words would you use to describe him?

2. What sorts of things make God happy? Angry? Impressed? What breaks his heart?

3. What do you want your relationship with God the Father to look like in a month? In a year? At the end of your life?

Scripture also tells us that as faithful followers of Christ, Jesus has made us his Bride, and thus he is our Bridegroom (Rev 19:7–9; 21:2, 9). What does marriage look like? Well, one byproduct of marriage is knowing the other person really well and working hard to take care of him. So, just as in any good marriage, we, as the Bride, must do this for our Bridegroom as well.

Prayerfully recall key moments from the life of Jesus. Feel free to go back to the Gospels and read through some of the stories anew.

4. How would you describe Jesus' personality? What strikes you about the way he interacts with others?

5. What makes Jesus happy? Angry? Impressed? What breaks his heart and makes him weep?

6. How can you bring a smile to Jesus' face today?

Pursuing God Like a Little Child
Prayer and Discussion Guide for Chapter Twelve

In any good relationship, we have to communicate regularly if we want to maintain a healthy friendship with the people we love. We call, text, Facetime, and (when all the planets align *juuuuust* right) we even get together in person to catch up with the ones we love. How else would we know what's going on in their lives? How would we know the things they're struggling with? The things they're celebrating? The ways we can pray for them? It's communication that keeps us connected, up-to-date, and bonded together. We know this is true about our family and friends, but how often do we think of it in relation to God?

Slowly read Isaiah 43:1–7. Imagine that God is speaking these words to you. Notice his tone of voice, his expression. Pay attention to the words or phrases that stand out to you.

1. How many times have your kids said your name today? (Just take an educated guess. No one can actually count that high.)

2. How many times has God said your name today? When were you best able to hear him? When you

couldn't hear him, what was it that drowned out his voice?

Just as God loves to call us by name, he also longs for us to say *his* name. He wants us to include him in everything we do.

3. Make a list of the kinds of things you do on a typical day (everything from chores and work to prayer and relaxation). Circle anything where God is already a "built-in" part.

4. Is there anything that surprises you about your list? What does God think of it? Does he have any suggestions to make?

5. Focus on the things that are not circled. What would it look like to invite God into these moments of your day?

6. Now pick something from your list that you especially want to live more intentionally in God's presence. What is one concrete way you can make God more a part of it? Ask the Lord to help you grow in this area.

Trusting God
Prayer and Discussion Guide for Chapter Thirteen

When I first heard the phrase, "Trust in Jesus," I had no idea what that meant. I mean, how can you trust something (or someone) that you can't even see? If someone had said, "Sit in that chair," I could look at the chair and understand how to sit in it. Even my toddlers can do that. They find *all sorts* of ways to sit in a chair. (In fact, I think they sometimes trust chairs more than they should.) As for me, I have to take a good look at the chair to be able to determine if it can hold my weight. Is it made out of paper? Is it made out of steel? Is it a chair for my kids' dolls? So on and so forth. In essence, I must know about and understand the chair before I can trust it.

That's exactly what we must do with God. We have to get to know him and understand him to be able to determine whether or not he can hold our weight. (Spoiler alert: he can!) But how can we take a look at God? Reading Scripture, receiving the sacraments, praying, and talking to other faithful Christians (perhaps even your pastor) is a great way to start.

1. Read 1 John 4:8. What does this passage teach us about the identity of God the Father?

2. Read 1 Corinthians 13:4–7. If God *is* love, we should be able to replace the word "love" with "God." When viewed that way, how does this passage from 1 Corinthians describe God?

3. What do these passages say to you about God's trustworthiness? Is anything in them new or surprising to you?

4. Think about all the areas of your life—physical, spiritual, and mental health; work; marriage;

finances; motherhood; relationships with family and friends; personal pursuits; etc. In what areas do you try to shoulder the burdens all by yourself? In which areas do you put your trust in God?

5. Read Joshua 4:1–7, 19–24. Are there any examples from your own life when you witnessed God working in big ways? Write them down in a prayer journal or share them with the group. That way, even in tough times, you can revisit these experiences and remember God's faithfulness, goodness, and power.

PART III: WHO ARE YOU?

Be Who You Really Are
Prayer and Discussion Guide for Chapter Nineteen

Have you stopped recently to consider what makes you, you? That's a silly question. Of course you haven't. You're a mom. We don't have time to think at all, let alone ponder such existential things. Half the time, we don't even know how we're doing. So much so, that when people ask, "How are you?" you find yourself rambling off a list of what your husband and kids have been up to. But where are *you* in the mix?

It's true that moms need to serve the family, but it's also important to remember that God made you *you* for a reason. You have your own strengths, skills, gifts, and also your own weaknesses and limitations. To best serve your family (and God!) and grow in your vocation of being a mother, it's important to be honest about all of these things so that you can play your role in your own skin.

Prayerfully read Proverbs 31:10–31. As you do so, try to see yourself reflected in the description in the passage.

1. How would you describe yourself—at your core—in five words?

2. What are some of the greatest strengths, skills, and gifts that God has given you? They can be anything. Physical abilities, personality traits, spiritual gifts, quirks, passions. You name it. (If you're discussing this in a group, you might want to take turns telling the others in the group what gifts and strengths you've seen in them. Point out their strengths and affirm their gifts. Sometimes it's hard to see those things for ourselves.)

3. How can you use your strengths, skills, and gifts to serve your family and God?

4. What are some of the most difficult parts of this stage of motherhood for you? How can you ask God or others for help with those areas that are more of a struggle for you?

Who Do You Imitate?
Prayer and Discussion Guide for Chapter Twenty-One

Humans have an amazing tendency to camouflage, and we're really good at mimicking what we see. (If you don't believe me, just watch little siblings when they're around their big siblings.) I often tell my kids that in everything in life, they have two choices: they can choose God or they can choose "not God." The same is true with who we mimic. We only have two choices. We can mimic God or we can mimic "not God."

Prayerfully read 1 Corinthians 13:4–7, considering how we are called to imitate God through each of the attributes of love described in this passage. Pay attention to the words that stand out to you and what stirs within you when you read them.

1. Which of the attributes in the 1 Corinthians passage do you reflect most clearly? In other words, in what ways are you God's mini-me?

2. Which attributes in the passage do you struggle most to emulate?

3. Besides your kids (because let's be real, they're always there), who else do you surround yourself with? Do the people around you reflect God or "not God"?

4. Have you ever considered that the characters from our favorite books, shows, and music also

influence our spiritual well-being? Take a moment to think about how the media you consume affects your spirit and your relationship with God. In what ways does it help you learn to imitate him better? Is there anything about the media you consume that you feel called to change?

God Created Us Body and Soul
Prayer and Discussion Guide for Chapter Twenty-Four

We might be tempted to focus more on either our soul or our body. But the truth is that they are equal counterparts: both are gifts from God, and they work together to help us experience him fully and share him fully. They are both worthy of our attention and care.

Ask the Holy Spirit to be with you, and then read through 1 Corinthians 6:19–20 and Deuteronomy 4:9.

1. Do you find that you tend to focus more on either your soul or your body?

2. Do you find that one—your body or your soul—is easier or more difficult to take care of than the other? What are some challenges you face in taking care of them?

3. How can you take care of your body as if you were going to live forever?

4. How can you take care of your soul as if you were going to die tomorrow?

PART IV: YOU CAN HAVE IT ALL
WITHOUT WAITING "UNTIL THEY'RE OLDER"

Praying While You're In The Trenches
Prayer and Discussion Guide for Chapter Twenty-Five

When my husband and I first started dating, we talked every single day. We shared our loftiest hopes, our greatest fears, our most embarrassing weaknesses, and our most miserable failings. We bared our souls to one another. And because of this, I actually liked him *more*. Then we got married and had babies, and all at once, that precious time together came to a screeching halt.

Now, five kids into marriage, we've learned to survive on texts and glances. We live for inside jokes and one-liners and belly laughs. Touches of the hand. Kisses on the forehead. These little connections remind us that we're not alone or forgotten.

The same is true with my prayer life, I've discovered. Instead of frequent, hours-long, soul-bearing talks with God, my relationship with him is maintained by short prayers and loving glances. These little connections remind me of my love for Jesus and also remind me that I'm still loved by him.

1. What does prayer mean to you? When you think about praying, what does it look like to you?

2. Have you noticed any differences in your prayer life since becoming a mother? How has it changed?

3. Read 1 Thessalonians 5:16–18, Philippians 4:6–7, and Romans 8:26. What do these verses teach us about prayer? What do they say to you about how to pray as a mom?

4. How can you schedule "dates" with God to have those longer, deeper conversations? How can you incorporate short prayers and loving glances during those in-between-dates times?

5. When you don't have lengthy time to be alone with God, how can you invite your kids, husband, or entire family to pray together?

What Are You Willing to Work Hard For?
Prayer and Discussion Guide for Chapter Twenty-Eight

When you're in the trenches, it can be hard to have priorities. Or interests. Or a life. But just because it's hard doesn't mean it's impossible. And also, just because it's hard doesn't mean it's *bad*. I often tell my kids that if something isn't worth working hard for, it's not worth having. That really grinds their gears, but it makes them start trying harder if they want something badly enough. The same is true with us. We must figure out what's most important to us and be willing to work hard for it.

Prayerfully read Hebrews 12:1–2 and 1 Corinthians 9:24, asking God for the grace of perseverance in your spiritual life.

1. What, or whom, do you consider worth working hard for? Jesus? Your husband? Your children? Your health? Physical fitness? Friends? A job or career aspiration? A particular hobby or passion?

2. Think about how you live every day: the tasks you do, the people you surround yourself with, the way you speak and act. What do you work the hardest for every day?

3. Is there anything on your list from Question 1 that you would like to make more of a priority? Or is there anything that's not on your list that you feel inspired to add? What would it look like to work hard for those things?

Here's the reality: life is hard. No matter what, you're going to have to work hard to get through it. For years, I chose not to go to daily Mass because it would've been too difficult with little kids. But in truth, I was going to have to work hard even if I stayed home. Because that's motherhood. As moms, we're constantly working. Constantly serving. Constantly running ourselves ragged. But if you're going to be spinning your wheels anyway, why not do so in acts of worship? As hard as it can be to keep faith a priority, it's worth the hard work because it fills us up with the strength we need to meet all of motherhood's demands.

4. What are some of your favorite spiritual practices? Are there any of these that you wish you could do more of? How can you incorporate those activities into your normal routine?

5. How can you incorporate spending time with Jesus in the Eucharist into your life more frequently?

6. What are you willing to risk or endure to be present at Mass?

Experiencing God Through Our Bodily Senses
Prayer and Discussion Guide for Chapter Thirty

One funny thing about children is that they require lots of different avenues of learning. They need to see, hear, touch, taste, and experience *everything*. So if we want to foster a rich faith life in our children, we have to give them opportunities to see, hear, touch, taste, and experience it themselves. You have the power to give them all of those things. Let them see and hear you pray—then let them pray with you. Let them touch your Bible and flip through it with you—then let them read some passages with you. Carry religious items with you and let your kids examine them and ask questions about everything. Take your family to Mass and let them get a good whiff of the incense. However you decide to immerse yourself in your faith, bring your children along for the ride and let them experience it, too.

Read 1 John 1:1–4, Deuteronomy 6:6–7, and Proverbs 22:6, asking God to enlighten you about the ways he reveals himself through the material world and to help you share what you learn with your children.

1. What are some ways you experience God through each of the five senses?

2. God has given us the sacraments as tangible signs of his grace working in us. How have the sacraments helped you experience God through your senses? How might this change the way you think about the sacraments?

3. What are some ways you can help bring your children to know and experience God through their senses?

Acknowledgments

They say it takes a village to raise a child, and that's true. What they *don't* tell you is that it also takes a village to write a book. Thanks be to God, I have the best village a girl could ask for, and a village like that deserves to be thanked.

First and foremost, I want to give a huge thanks to Dawn and Greg Luna, my mom and dad, who not only put up with me through the trenches of parenthood (poor souls), but still put up with me today. Thanks for allowing me to dream, read, and hide in my quiet, introverted bubble, stuffing my face with mini-Oreos while writing books throughout my adolescence, and for always being some of my most loyal readers. How could I possibly repay you for the life you've given me? I can't. So, I hope you'll accept this measly paragraph along with my genuine and unending thanks.

Thanks to Roy and Jimmie Detraz, my grandparents, who served as second parents to me. I cherished every weekend at your house. Grandma, thanks for all the books you read me as a kid and the way you cuddled up with me to tell me all about the books you'd been reading. You single-handedly inspired my love of stories. I'll love you and Pawpaw forever and ever.

Thank you to Mike and Kristine Gillespy—the best in-laws the world has ever seen—who've no doubt put more blood, sweat, and tears into this manuscript than I have by taking care of my kids so I could go sit in silence, drink coffee, and stare at my laptop. Every day, I thank God that I got to marry into your family.

To my soul sisters who've walked side by side with me through these trenches: I couldn't do life without you. I've learned so much about how to be a better mother because of you. Mary Pat Reed, thank you for being my go-to prayer warrior, hype-man, and motivator. The richness of your Catholic faith is so incredibly beautiful. Maddie Muzyka, I need you in my life. The way you mother is inspiring and our belly laughs give life to my soul. Virginia Collier, my sweet sister-in-law, I always wished to have a sister like you. Now, praise God, I get to have one. How did I get so lucky? Melanie Smeragliuolo, I sure hit the jackpot with you. You've shaped the way I approach motherhood perhaps more than anyone else. Not to mention that you've read more terrible drafts of my work than anyone should ever have to endure. Lizeth Morris, I wouldn't be writing at all if not for you. Thanks for helping me get back in the writing saddle. Kellie Moore, my former-editor-turned-forever-friend, you made me fall in love with writing about my Catholic faith. Thank you for your constant kindness and encouragement, in writing and in life.

Big shout out to PBM acquisitions editor, Sr. Allison Regina Gliot, who believed in this manuscript from the get-go and then so sweetly shaped it into something better. Thank you also to my editor Courtney Saponaro who, with her profound wisdom and encouraging comments, miraculously made revisions fun. You both are brilliant, Catholic word wizards.

Thank you to my kids, who've literally provided me a book's worth of material. You constantly keep me on my toes, and I have no doubt you'll only continue to teach me more about God as you grow. Your life stories are my favorite stories in the world, and I'm so glad you allow me to have a front row ticket to watch them unfold every day.

To Kyle Gillespy—my biggest supporter, my best friend, the leader of our family and MVP of our marriage—I admire you, I respect you, and I love you more than I ever knew I could love anyone. Life is better when you're around. Thanks for keeping your feet on the ground so I can keep my head in the clouds.

And, of course, thanks be to God who swooped into these trenches to be with me, to guide me, and to teach me more about how to parent by giving me glimpses of the greatest Father who ever existed. I honestly don't know how anyone can survive these trenches without you, God.

And, lastly, to all you readers—whether you have children or not, whether you are a mother or father, whether your children are grown or still small—thank you. When you hold this book in your hands, you make all my childhood dreams come true.